Martin Maeller
Nervous Dust

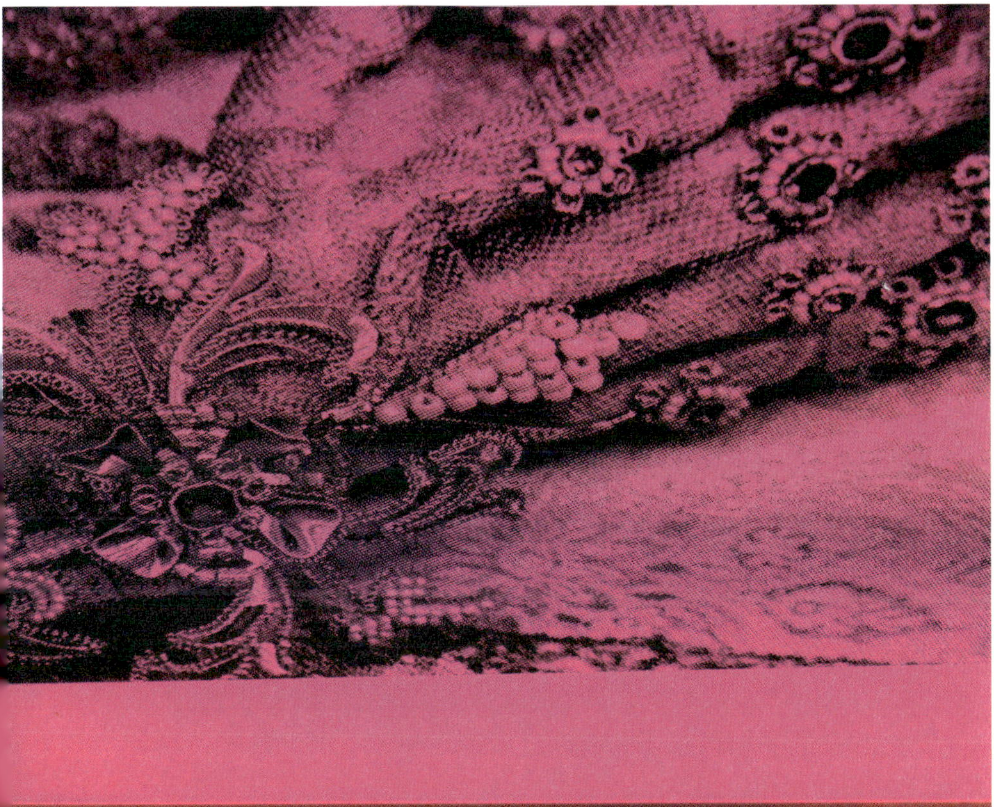

I see the stars, I am the same.
Darkness, say my name –
because you know, I will remain.

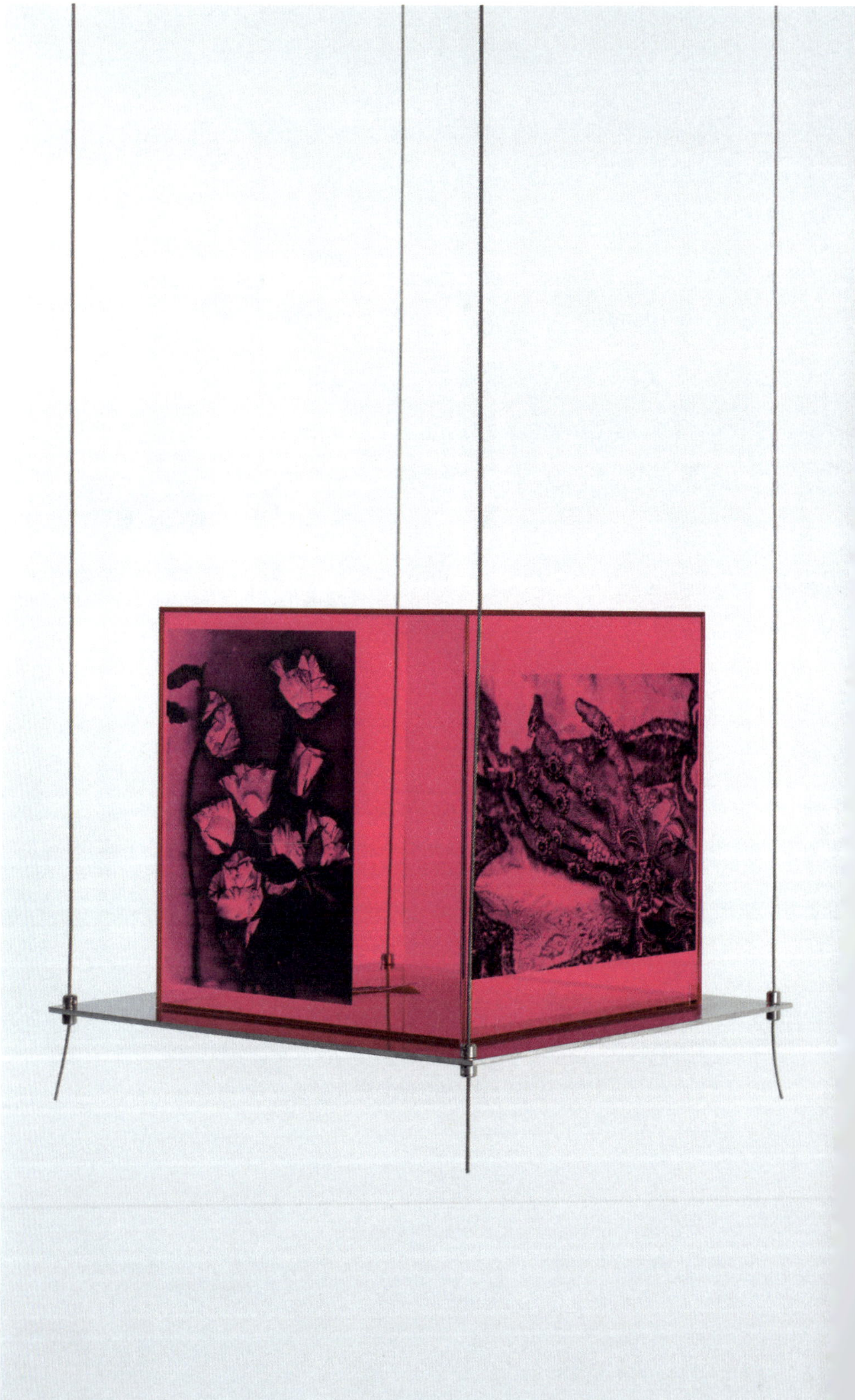

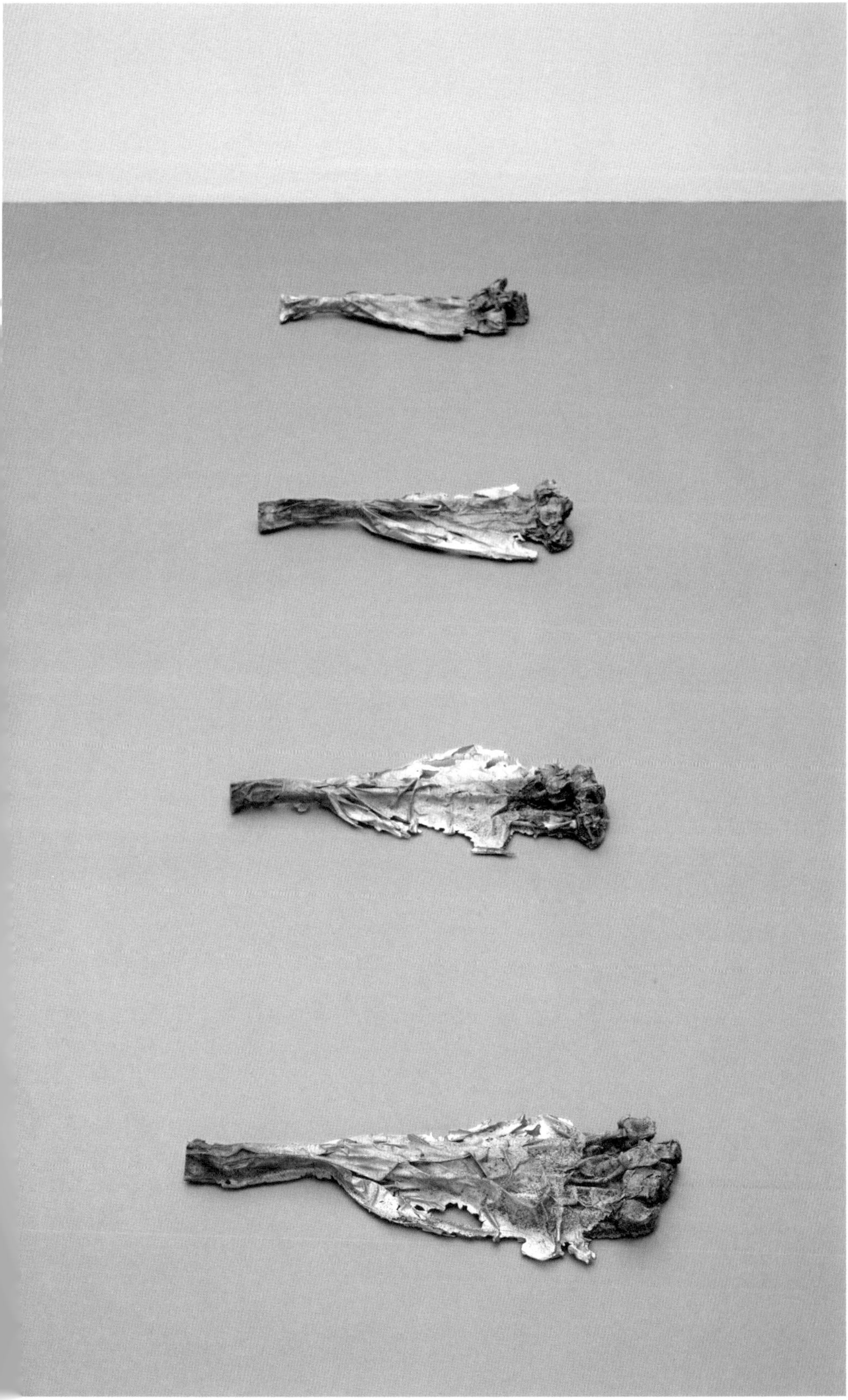

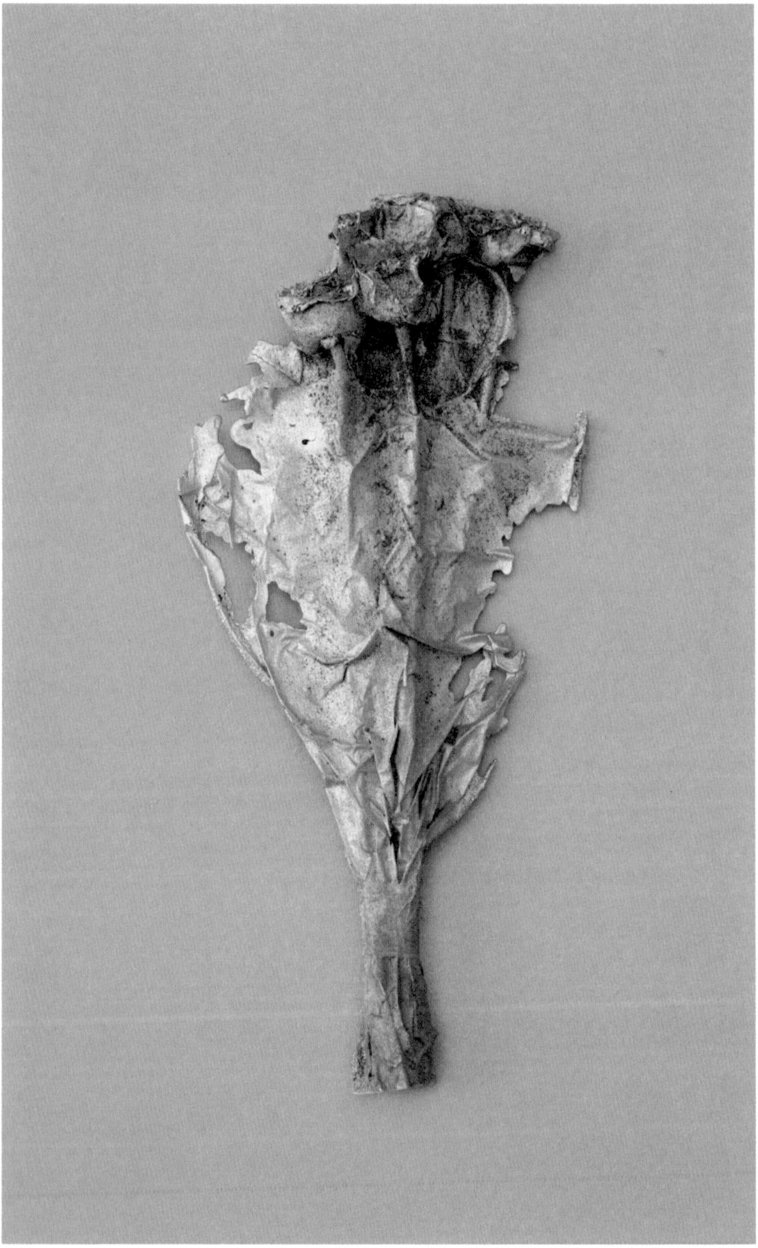

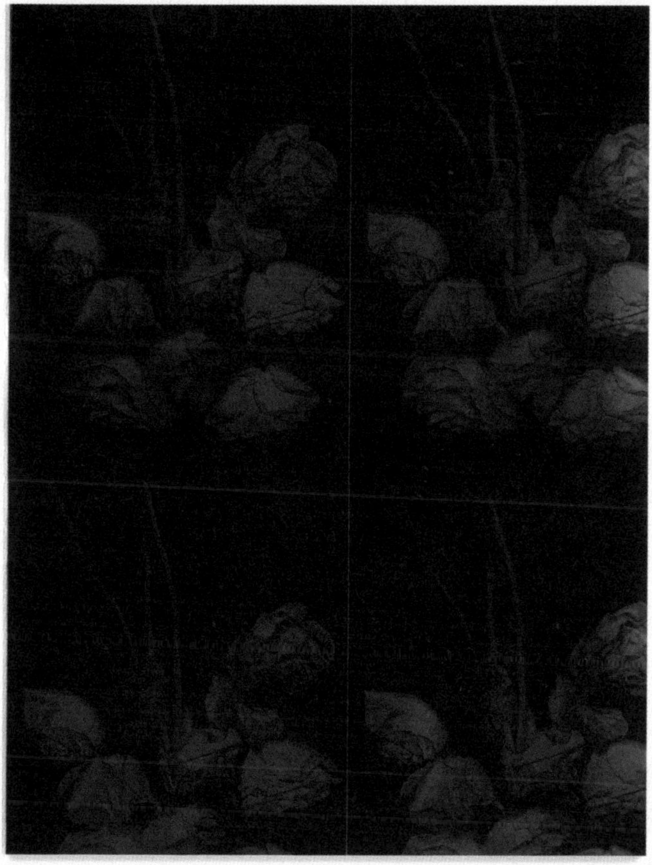

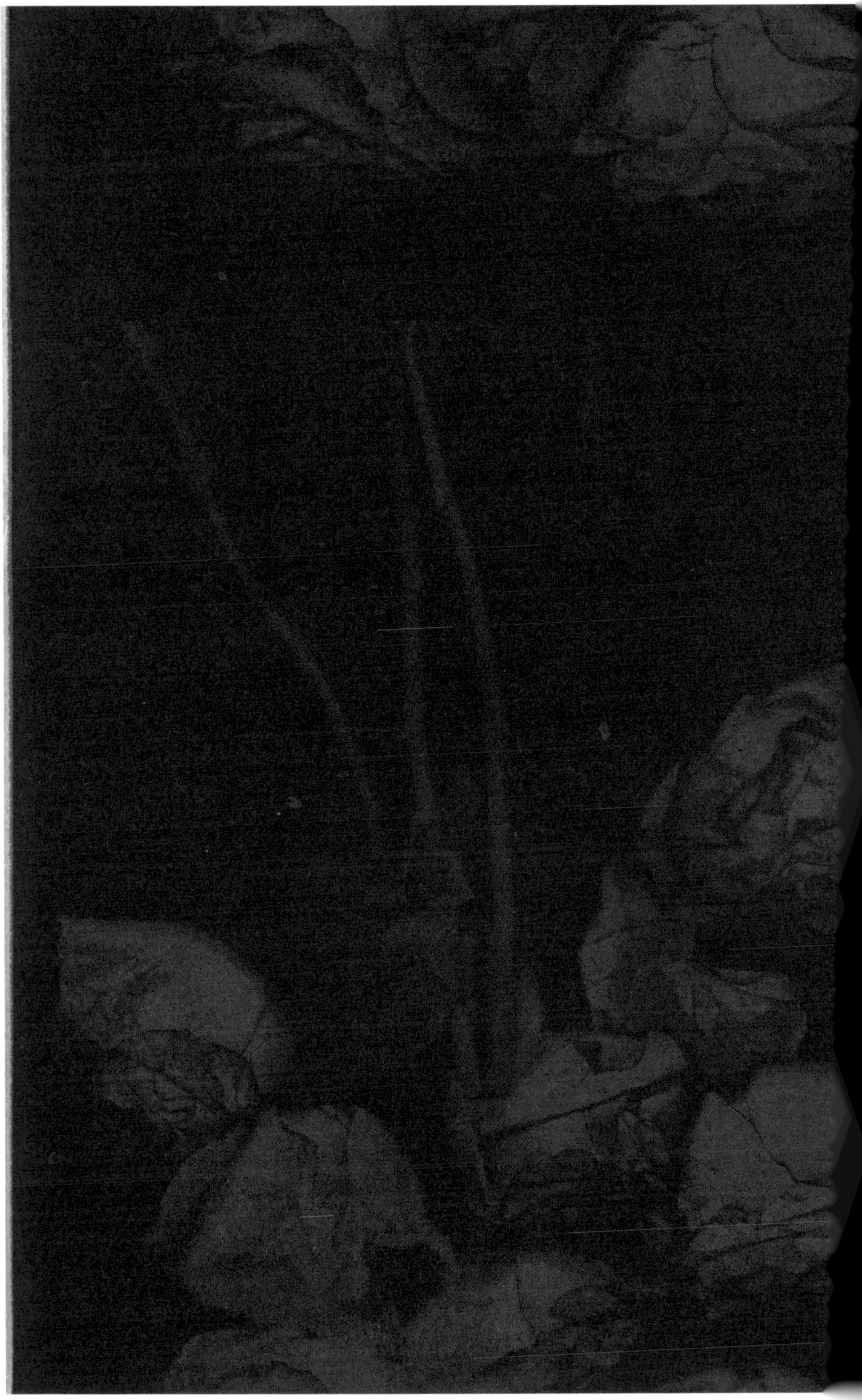

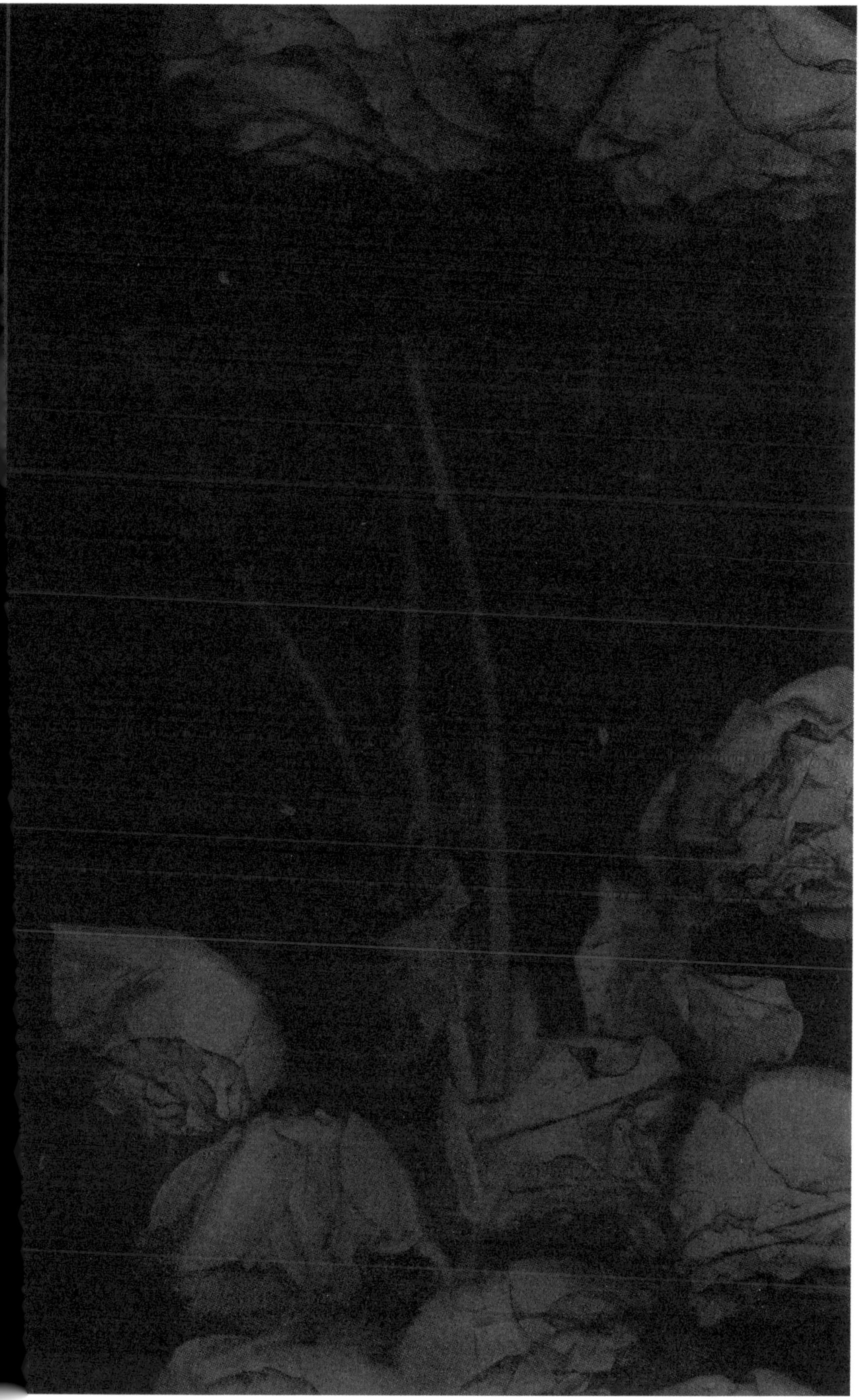

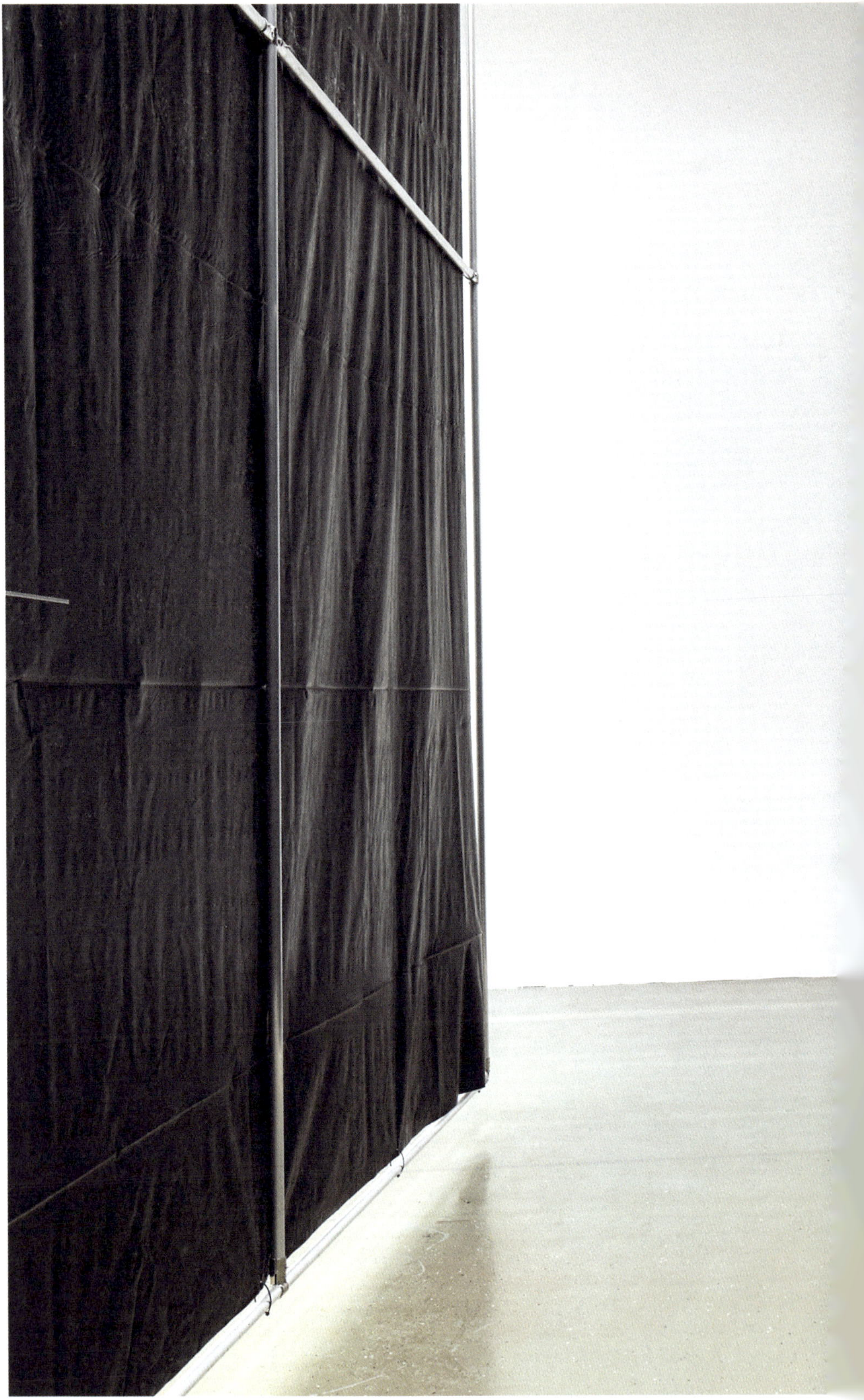

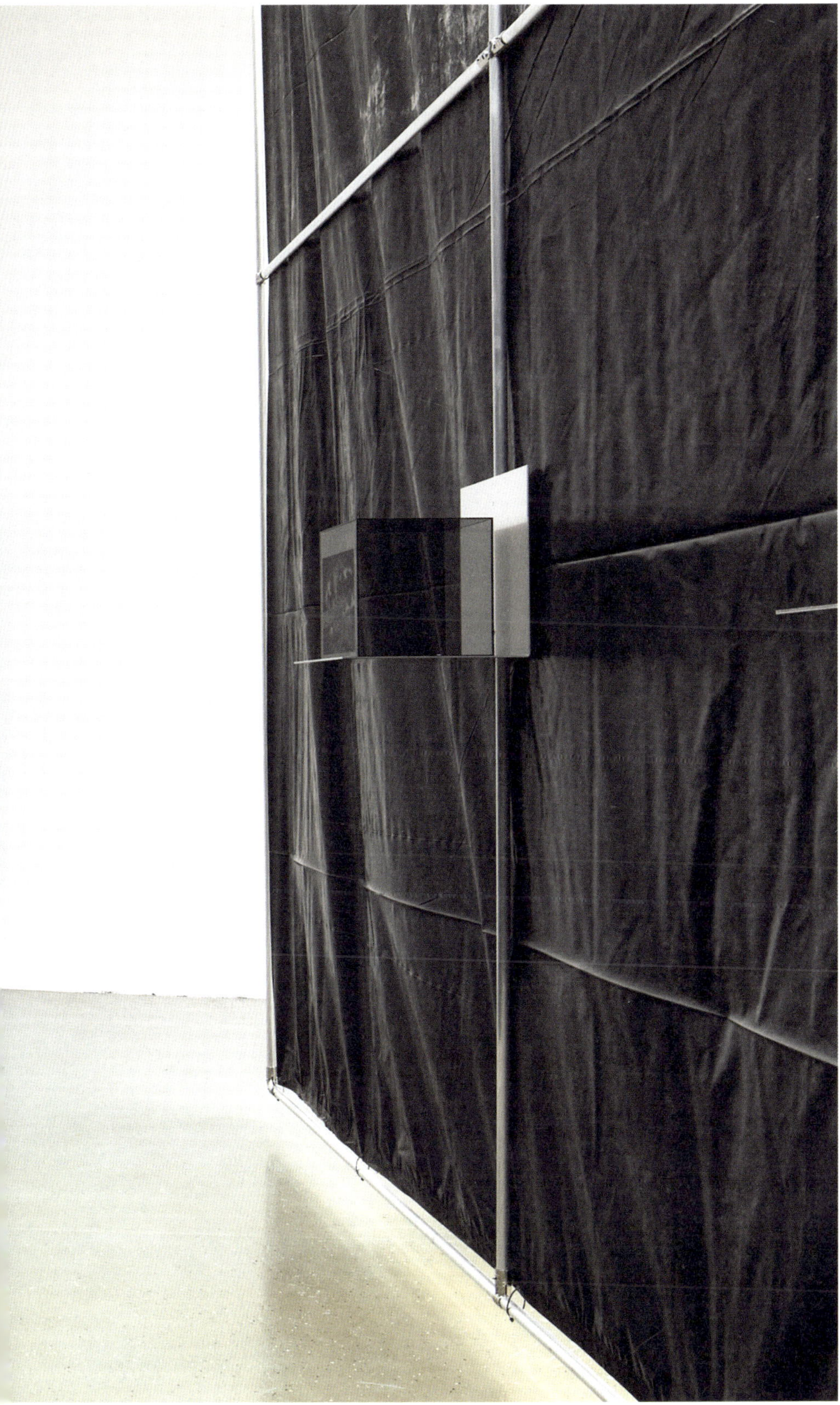

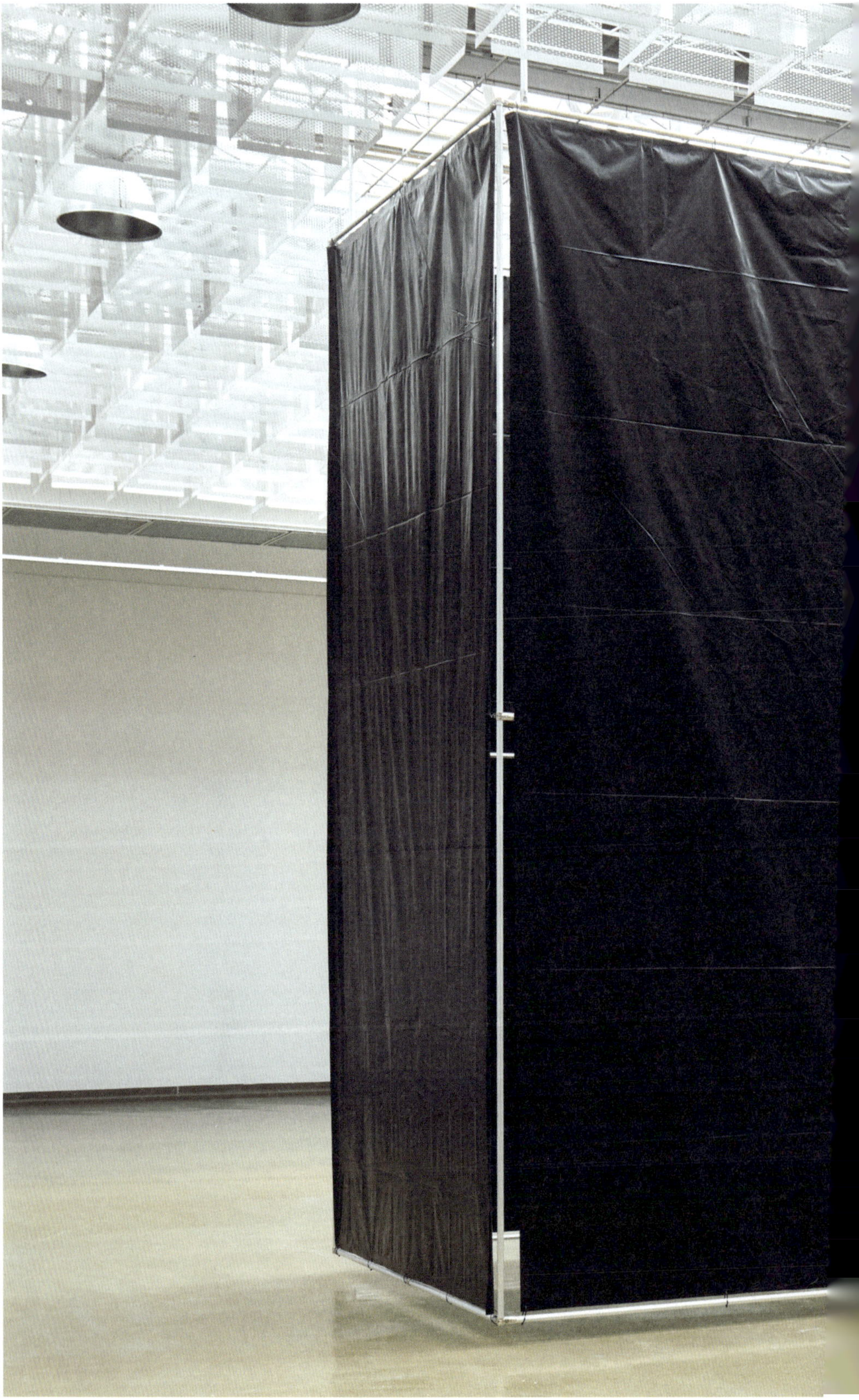

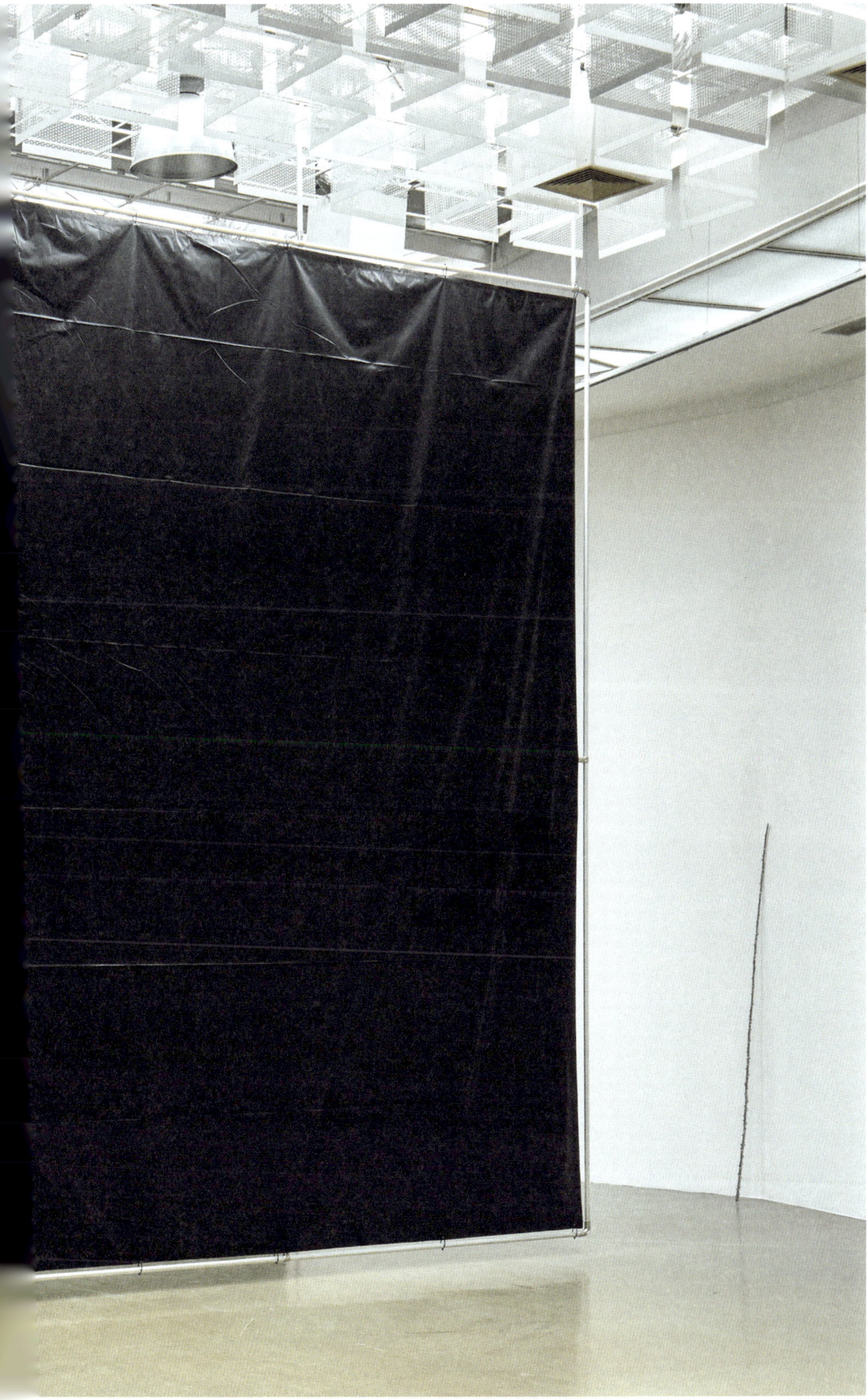

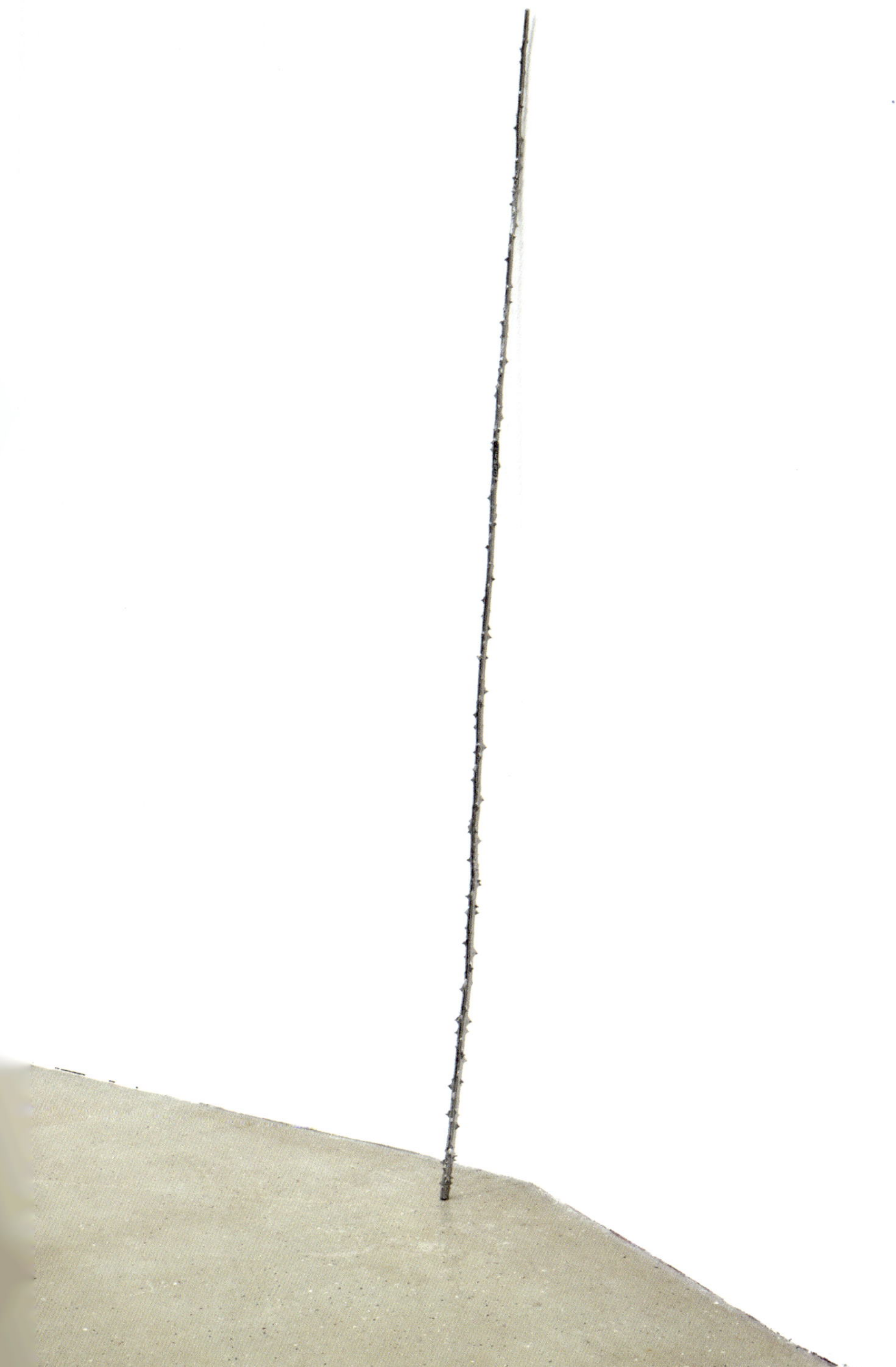

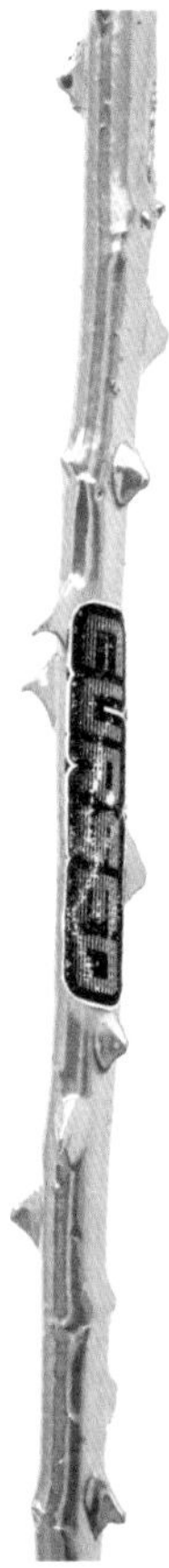

Considering that melancholy is a condition—a pathology, even—that some characterize as *asymbolique*, it is astonishing how much is written about it. But then again, one would be hard-pressed to just write about melancholy; it is not a topic. For the afflicted, it pervades everything. It fundamentally changes the perception of the world. What is written about it, is always also written *from* melancholy, as if language itself is intoxicated, as if the condition afflicts signs, words, and sentences.

Everything has been felt by someone else before. In Robert Burton's *The Anatomy of Melancholy* (1621), the scholar takes stock of possible causes of melancholy. Some are supernatural, like witches and magicians, while others are natural, like the constellation of stars, old age, or traits inherited from one's parents. Some are self-inflicted, such as poor diet and drunkenness. And then, Burton lists self-love, pride, and vainglory. The melancholic's vain conceit of their good qualities is an active cause. Like Narcissus, we admire, flatter, and applaud ourselves, writes Burton: "What's a city to a kingdom, a kingdom to Europe, Europe to the world, the world itself that must have an end, if compared to the least visible star in the firmament, eighteen times bigger than it?" The melancholic gets a feeling for the infinite—or not. Born under the sign of Saturn, melancholics have been cosmologically bound to that planet at least since the Middle Ages. Saturn emits particles that hold the entire world under its spell, like the black bile which permeates the body. Think of Saturn as the sun's nocturnal proxy, as a fearful, bitter, and lonely god without a throne.

Melancholy stands in the way of an age that tries to purge the metaphysical and attempt the impossible: to rid its own thinking of dark corners and establish a relentless regime of well-being as it sweeps the murky recesses. Melancholy is the profound homesickness for the dim spots, and this longing is forever disappointed, which is what makes it ache. Melancholy is Narcissus's hidden face, the other side of his self-love.

Sadness is the expression of a wounded primal self. But what's more, melancholy is about love—love for a lost object; that is, grieving for the mother-object, psychoanalysis tells us. Loving, and hating, because love is fear of loss of the other.

Perhaps among the most beautiful works created out of melancholy is composer John Dowland's inventory of tears—simply titled *Lachrimae*—from 1604. The music is at risk to be ridiculous if it weren't for the self-awareness in the titles of the slow-paced pieces: *old tears, new tears, sad tears*, he calls them, possibly tongue in cheek. Unlike Orpheus, whose music made gods, stones, and all of nature weep, Dowland does not draw iron tears from Pluto's cheek. Why are people drawn to sorrow? Perhaps it is an antidote to loneliness, when one's own sentiment is mirrored. Maybe it cleanses and has a cathartic effect.

Dowland's collection of songs prefigures something more modern. Like a pop album, it assembles sad pieces, and like an echo through the centuries, the repercussions are felt in music until our own day. The last of Dowland's pieces is called *Semper Dowland, semper dolens*—forever Dowland, forever in pain, simultaneously an assertion of self-pity, that special form of narcissism, and a lamentation of lost love.

I love, but even more I hate, and to not lose the other, I insert them into myself. But because I hate them, the other in me is a worse me. What's left out? The other. Unless, of course, as connected as melancholy is to self-love, one thinks of it as a form of cannibalism.

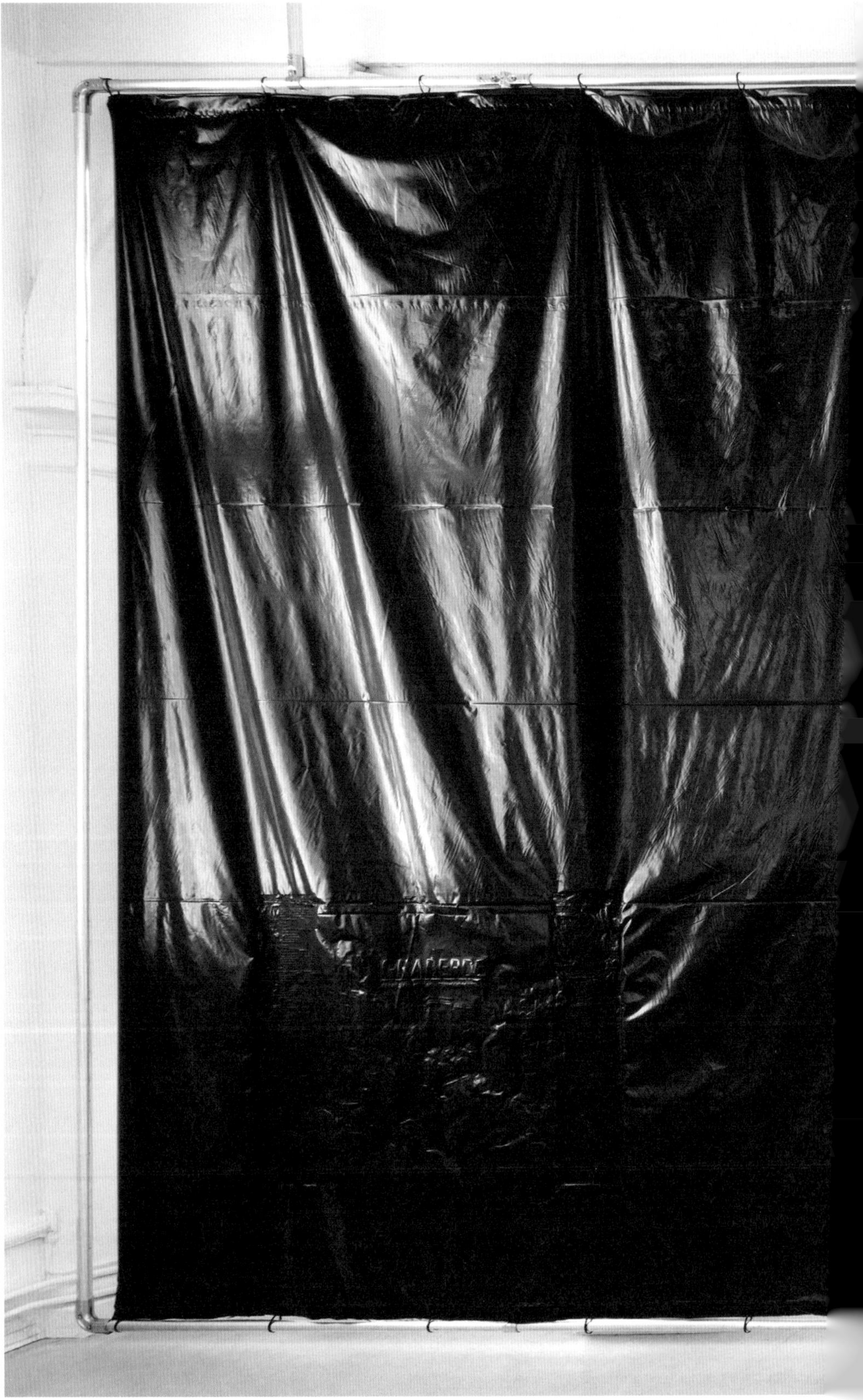

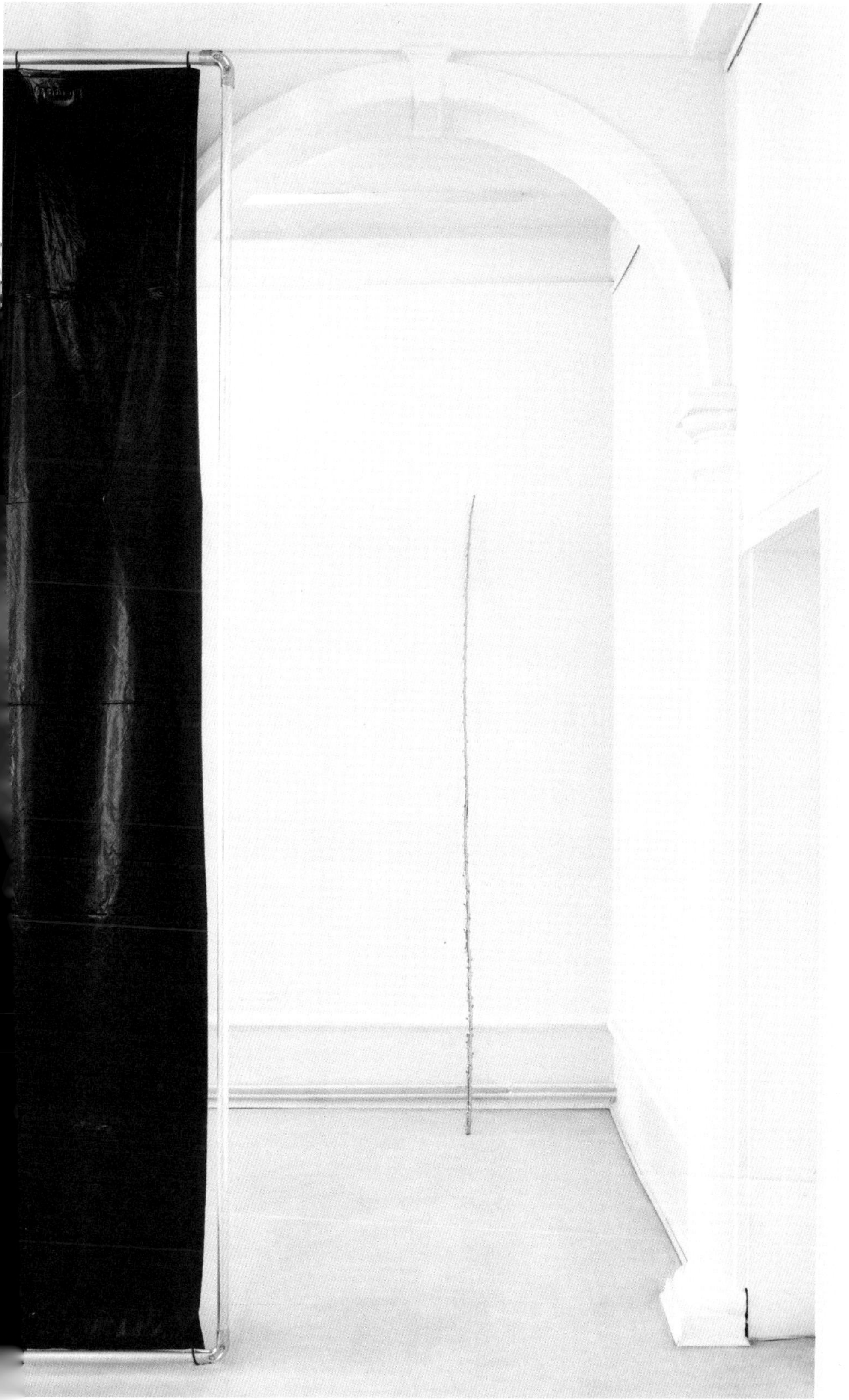

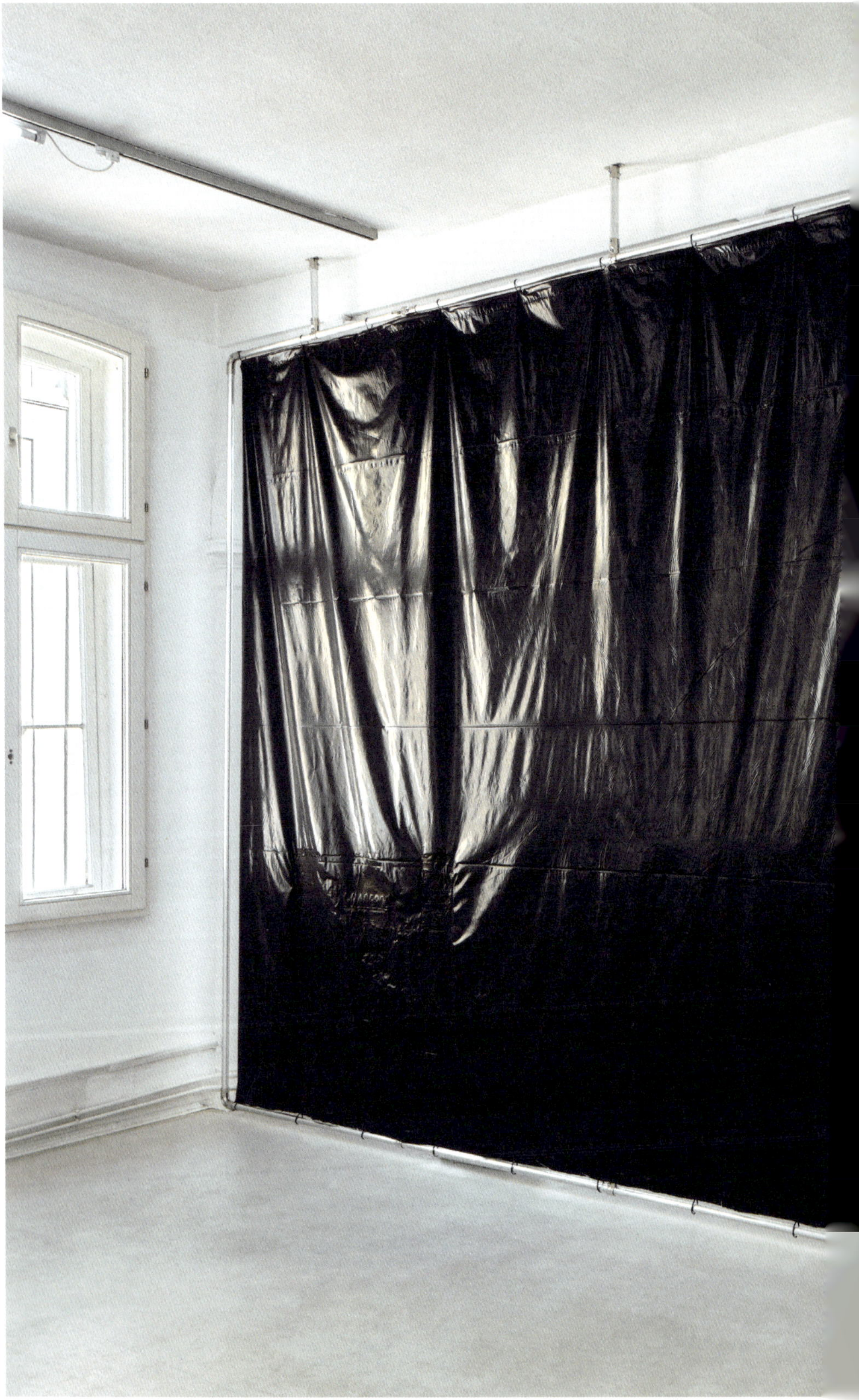

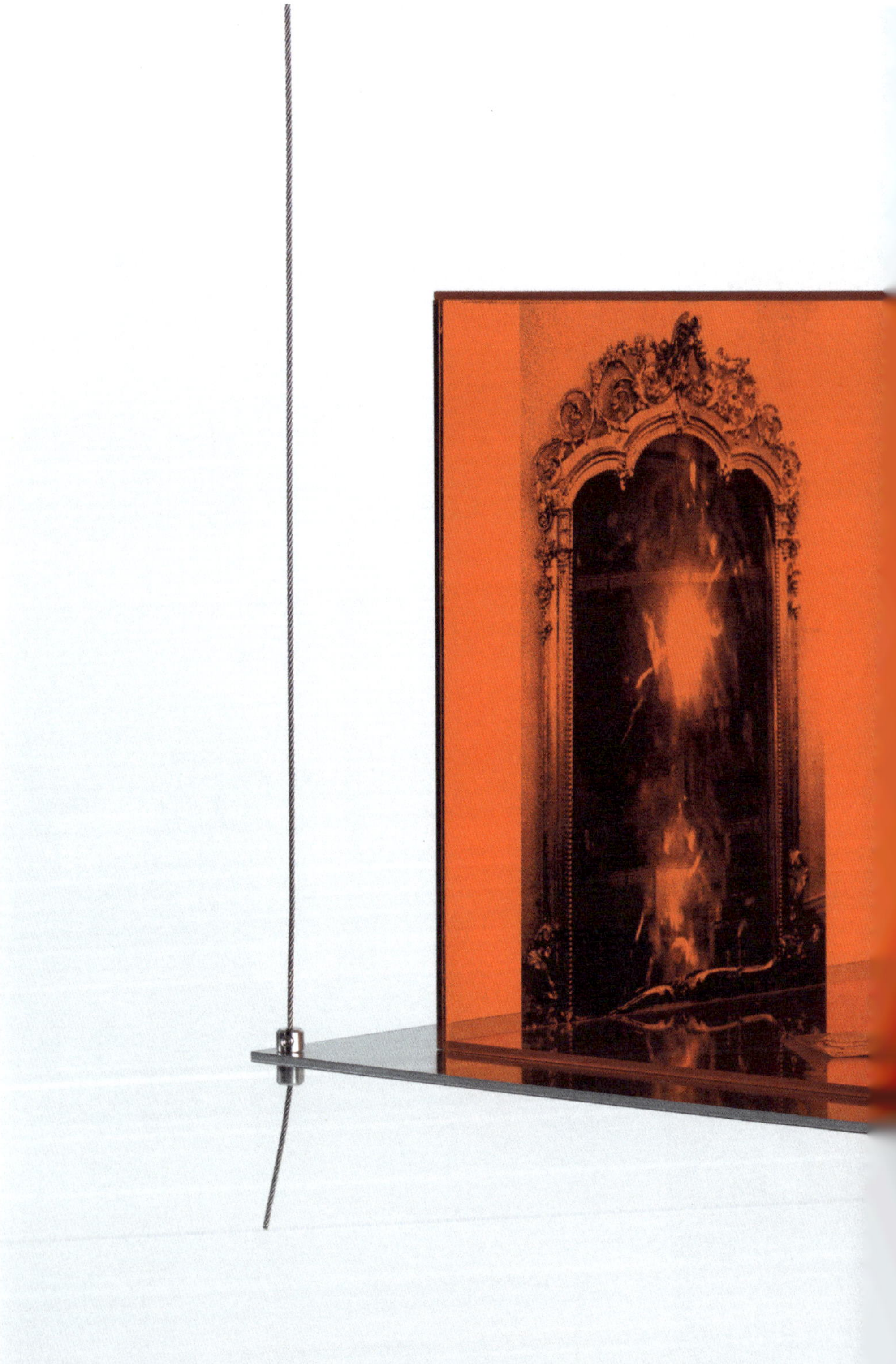

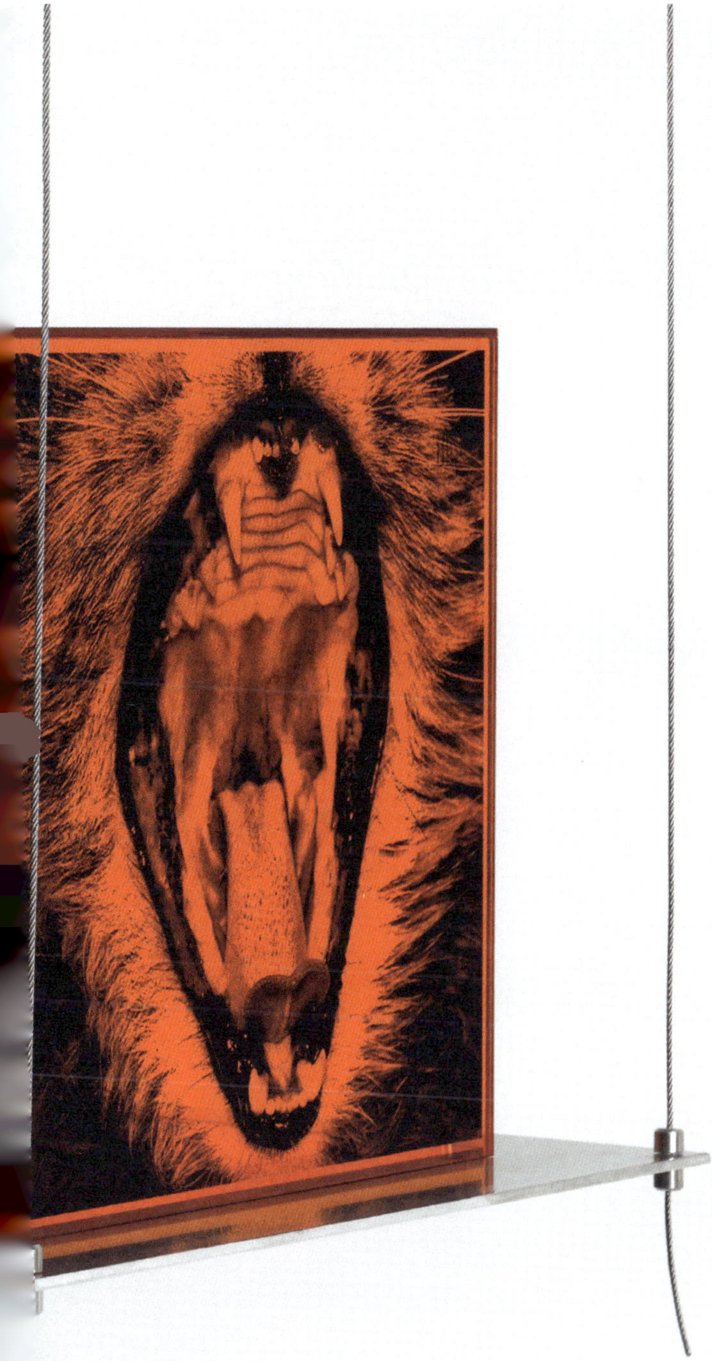

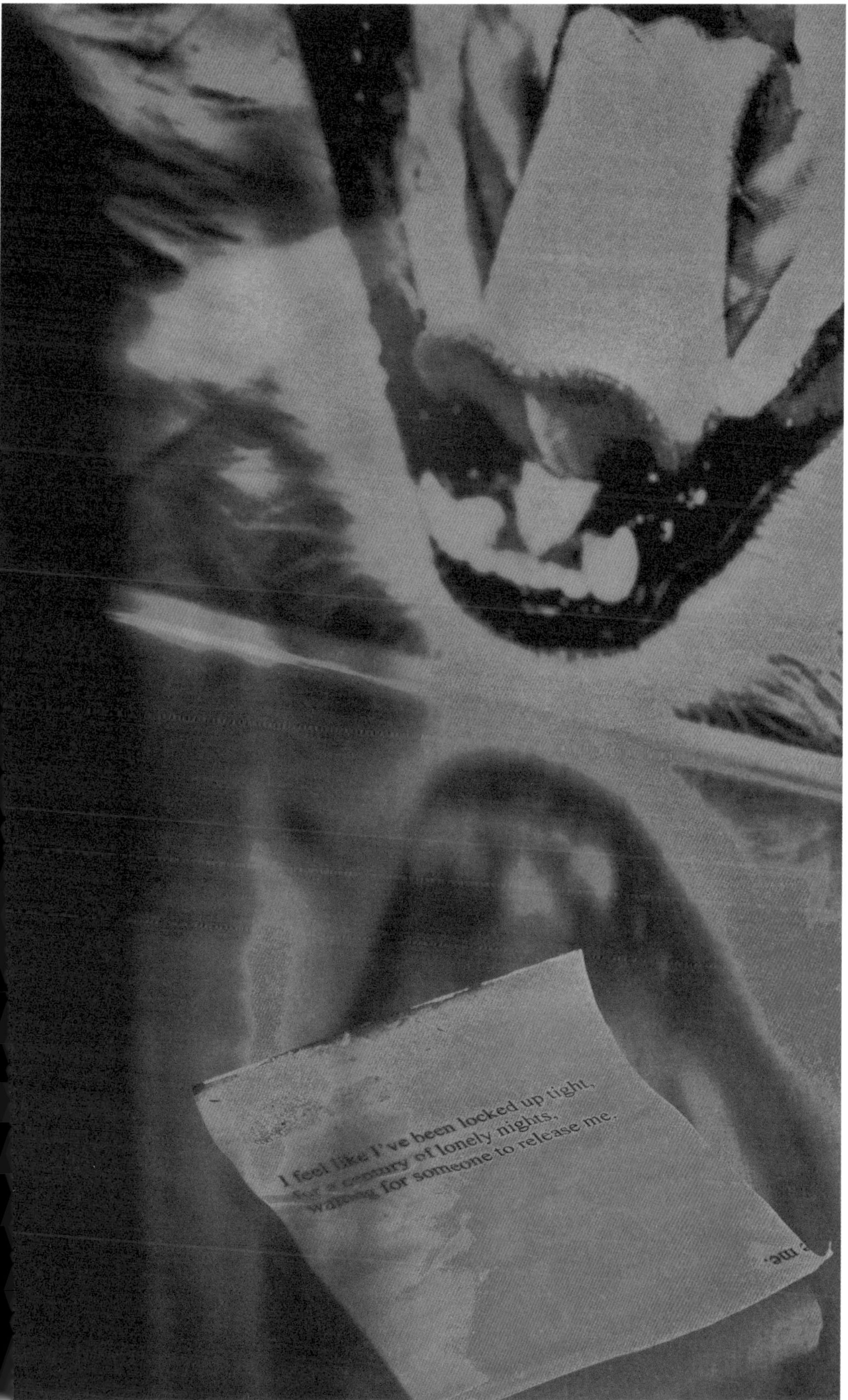
I feel like I've been locked up tight,
for a century of lonely nights,
waiting for someone to release me.

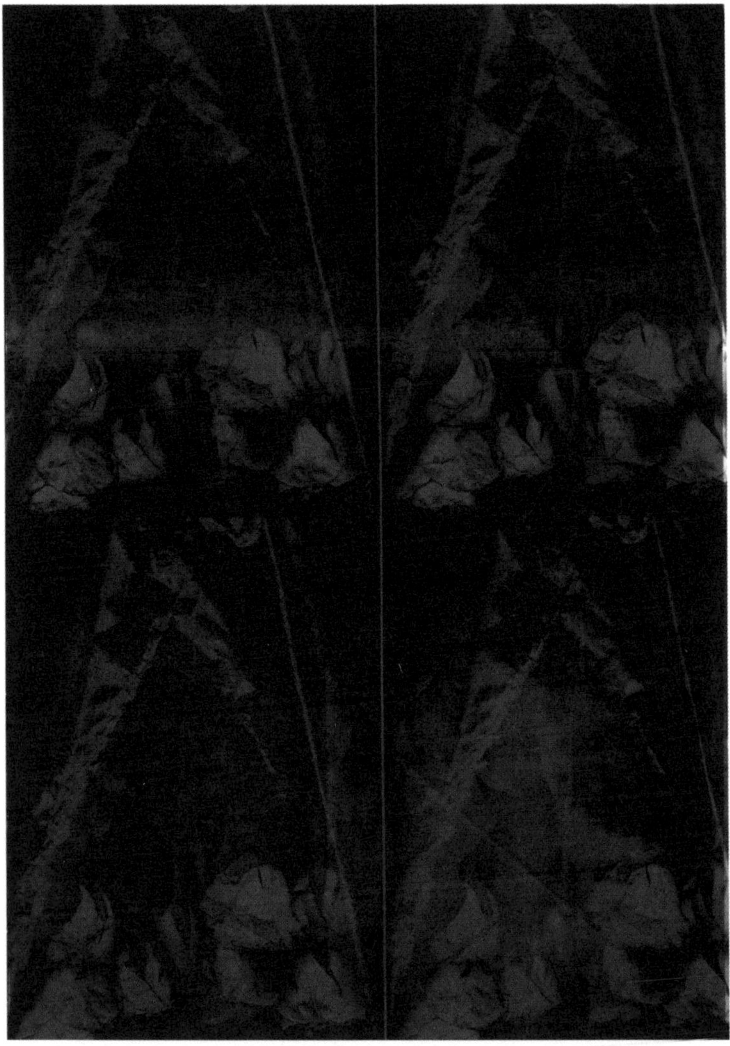

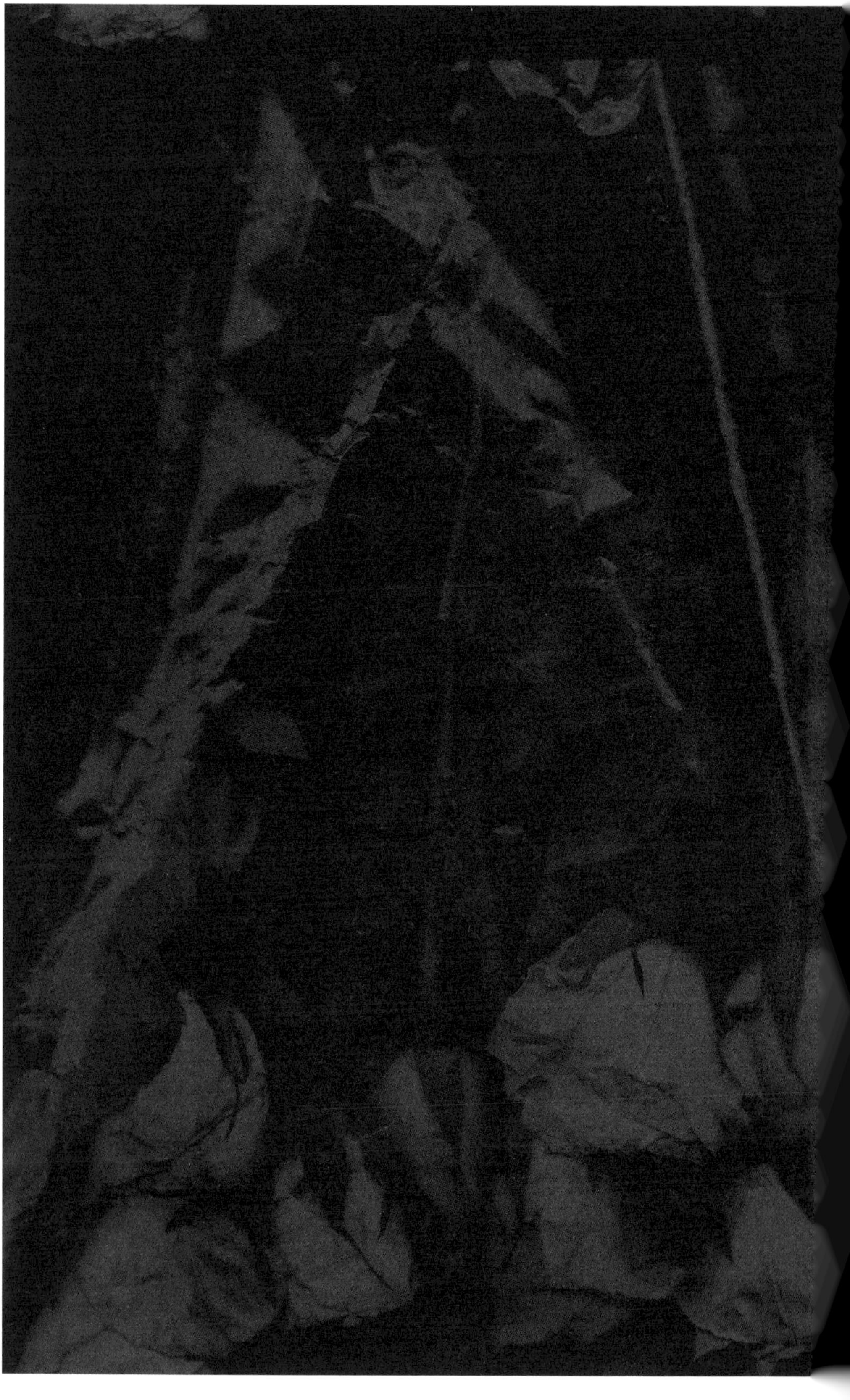

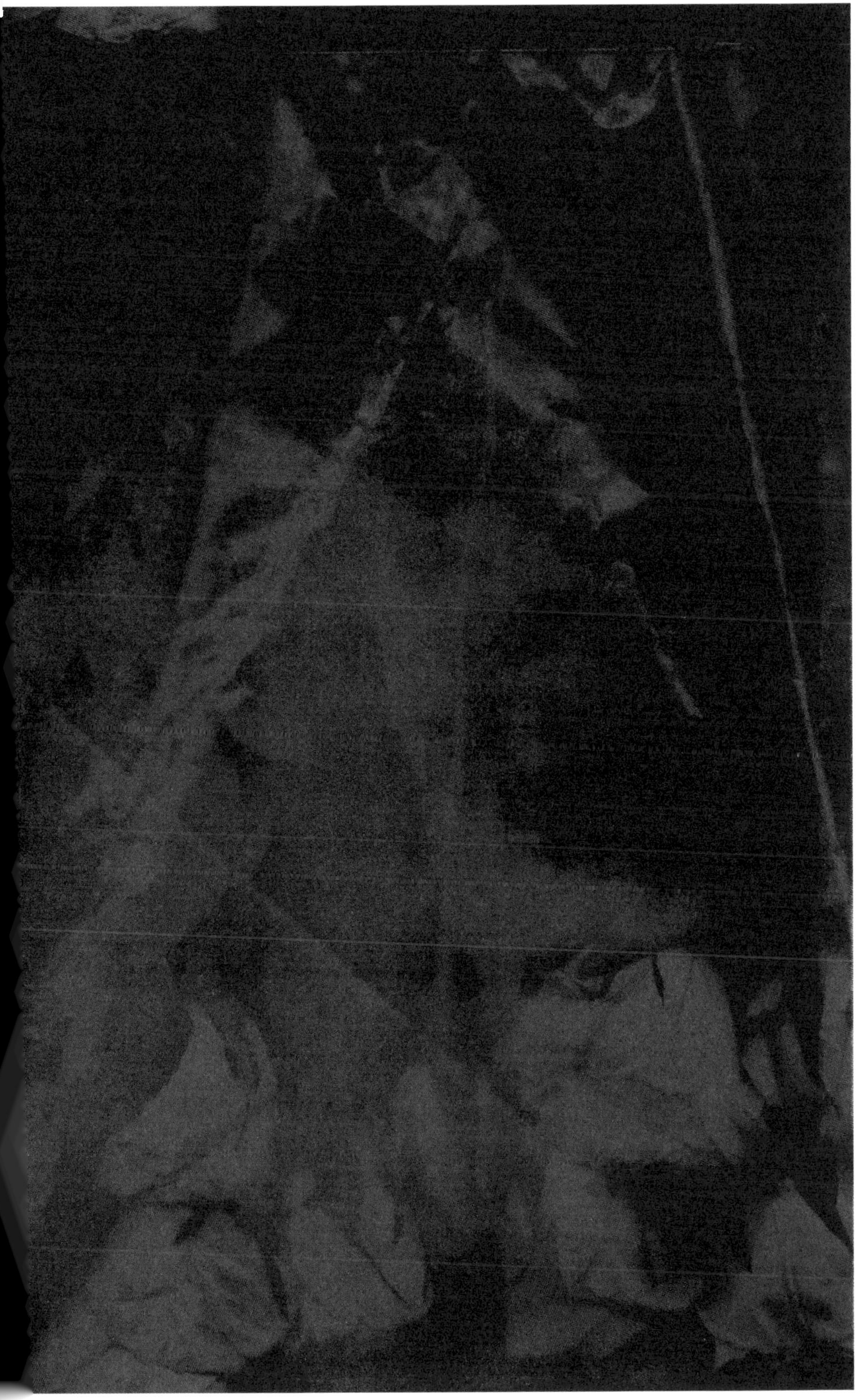

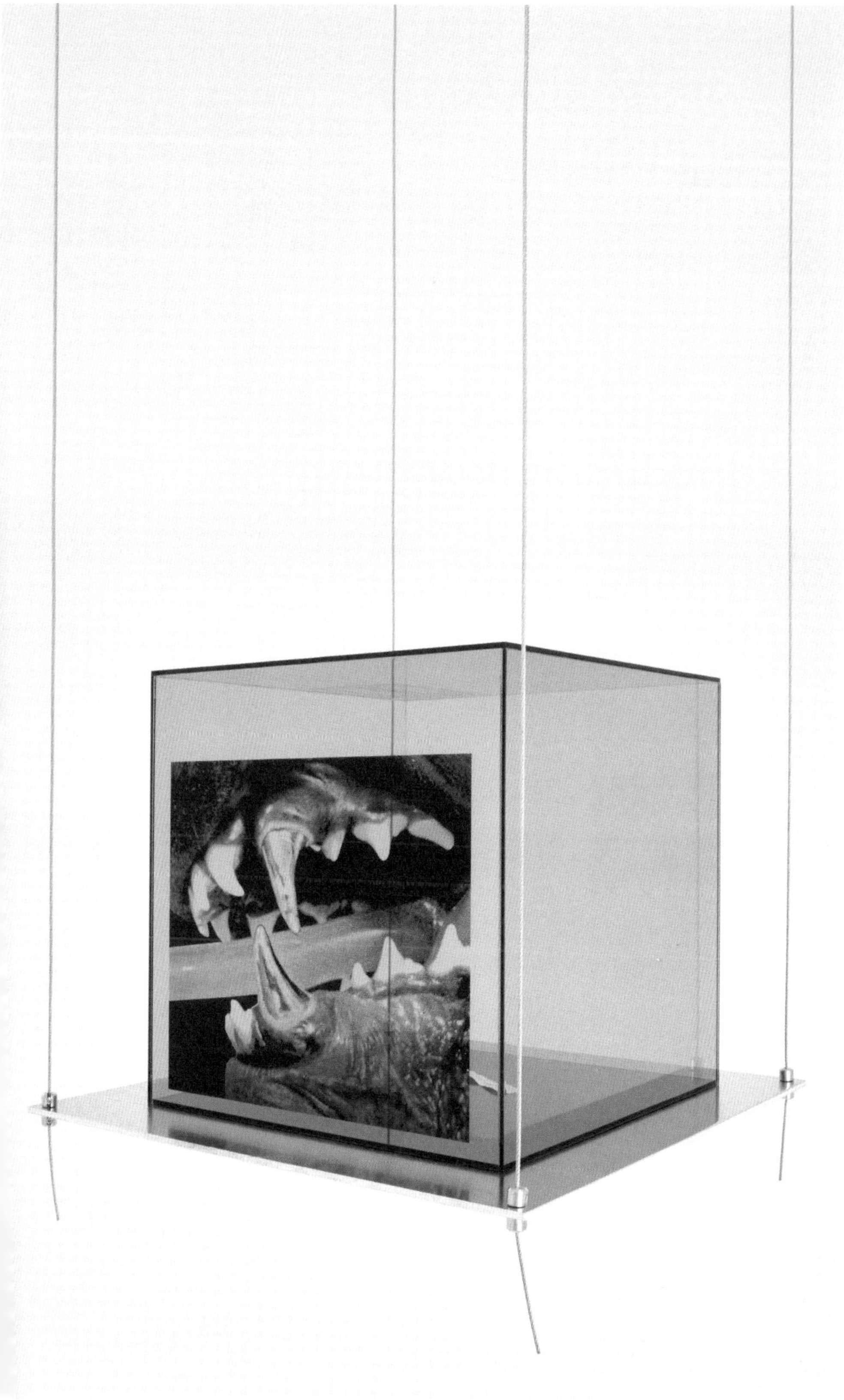

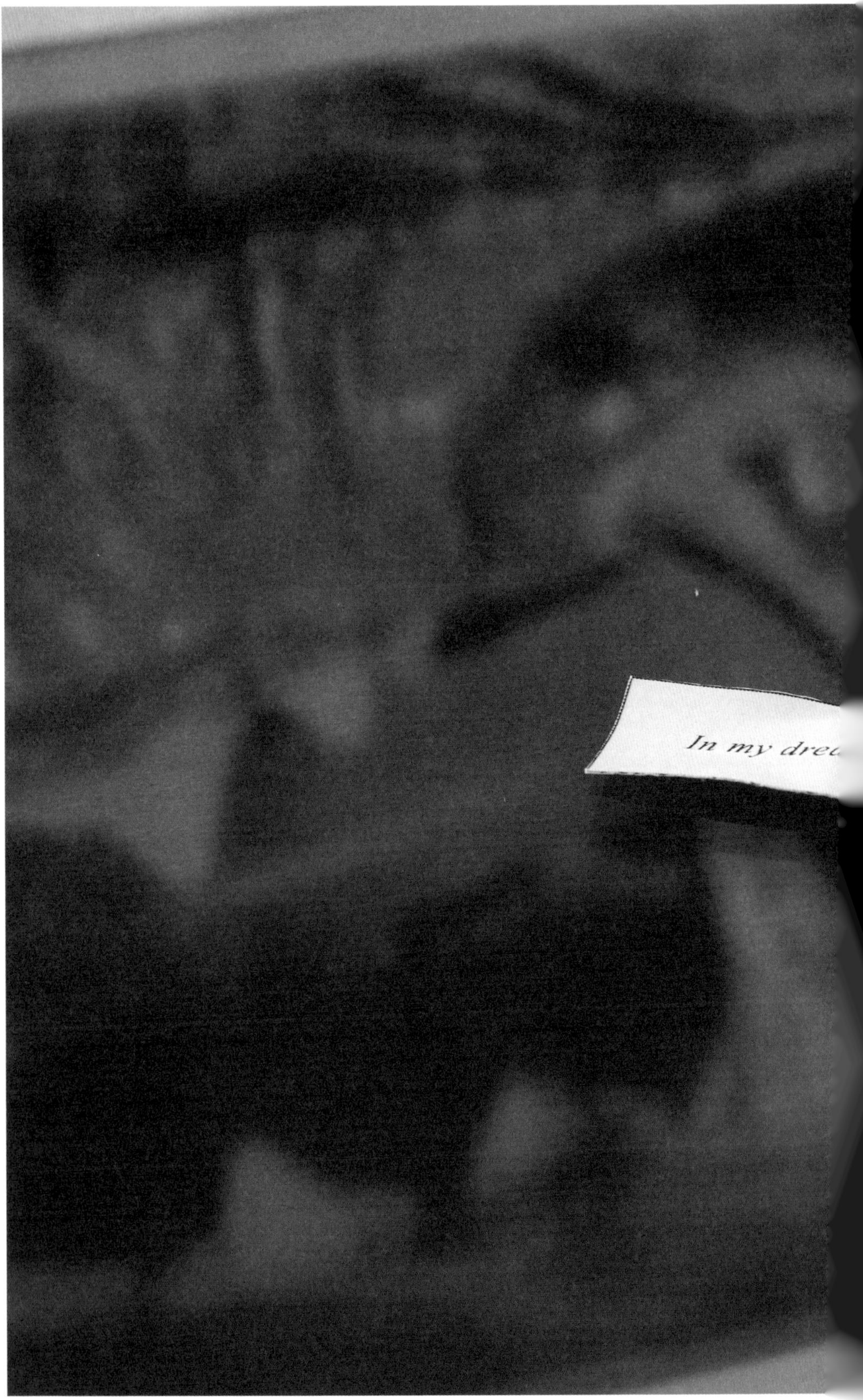
In my

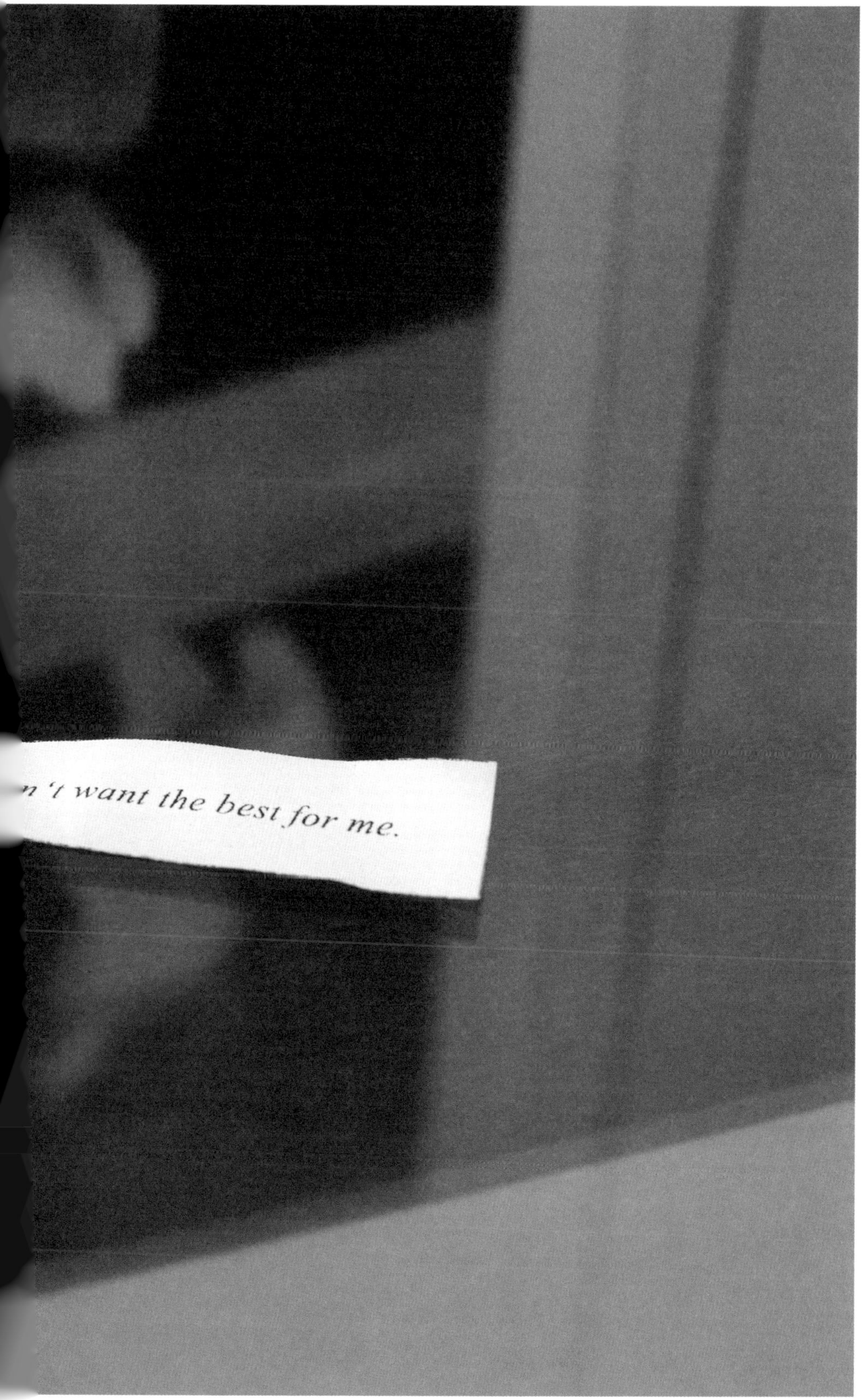
n 't want the best for me.

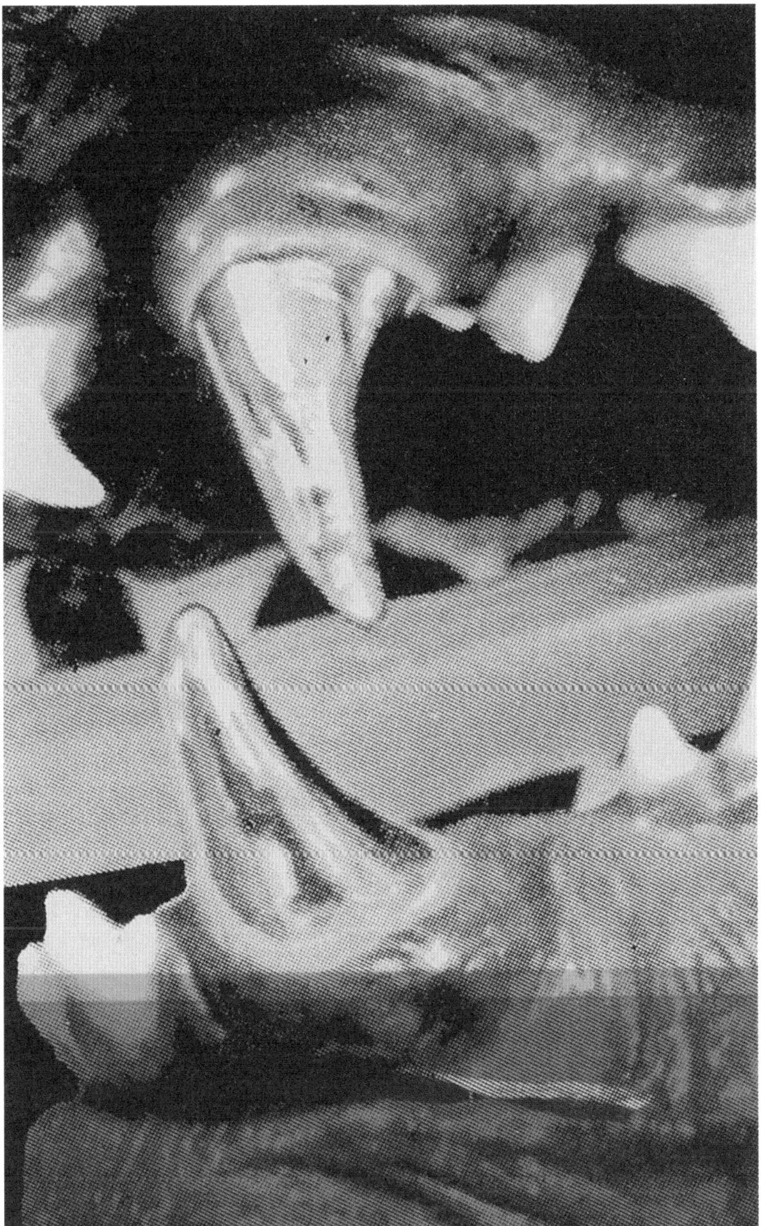

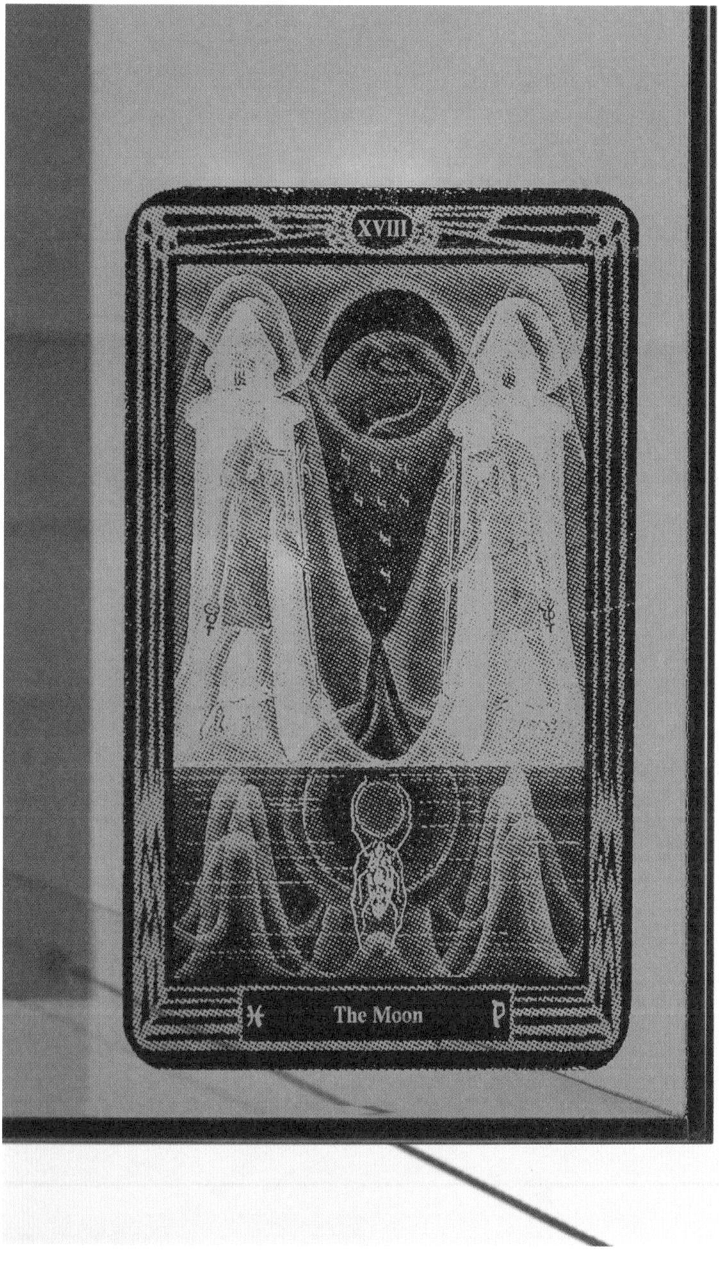
XVIII
The Moon

an opus on love
P. Staff

an opus on love no matter how destitute it is, i told my buddy that love is expansive
i ask my buddy, my exchange buddy how to express true uncertainty in a second
language but he didn't get it, he parroted it back to me, i said no i know i know, but—
i am certain that love can and will reorganise us re-constitute us, even
if you say, you have had to stop believing in it stop waiting on it stop relying on it
& i can't tell you how sad that makes me, what a letdown what a fool i am, i know it
no matter how much i say love is expansive, express uncertainty, again and again
that there are times you cannot rely on it and i cannot do it for you
a sadness overwhelmed me i have nothing left today you've gotta do better
you've gotta do better [deep breath]
love is an opus against death but not dying ,, maybe extinction—
against every extinction—even if you say you had to stop believing in it,, relying on it,,

maybe its true that no thing is ever another thing, you cannot illustrate or replace one for
another, i cannot replace you
creme de la creme, whirling view of a city, easter whip on love's landscape—
even if listed no metaphor is anything else, i know, no object no action literally
applicable,
but i will say it anyway,,

love is an opus, on suffering against extinction—a thing i cannot promise but will
promise you it is coming it is coming and it will not gird you, it will not change you
but it *will* change everything,, i am trying i am trying,
in the same way a settled layer of dust over everything
can change everything it is that; it is dust; it is pollen in every pore
and it hurts, i am sorry it hurts, i am sorry and it is coming
and i am suffering for it

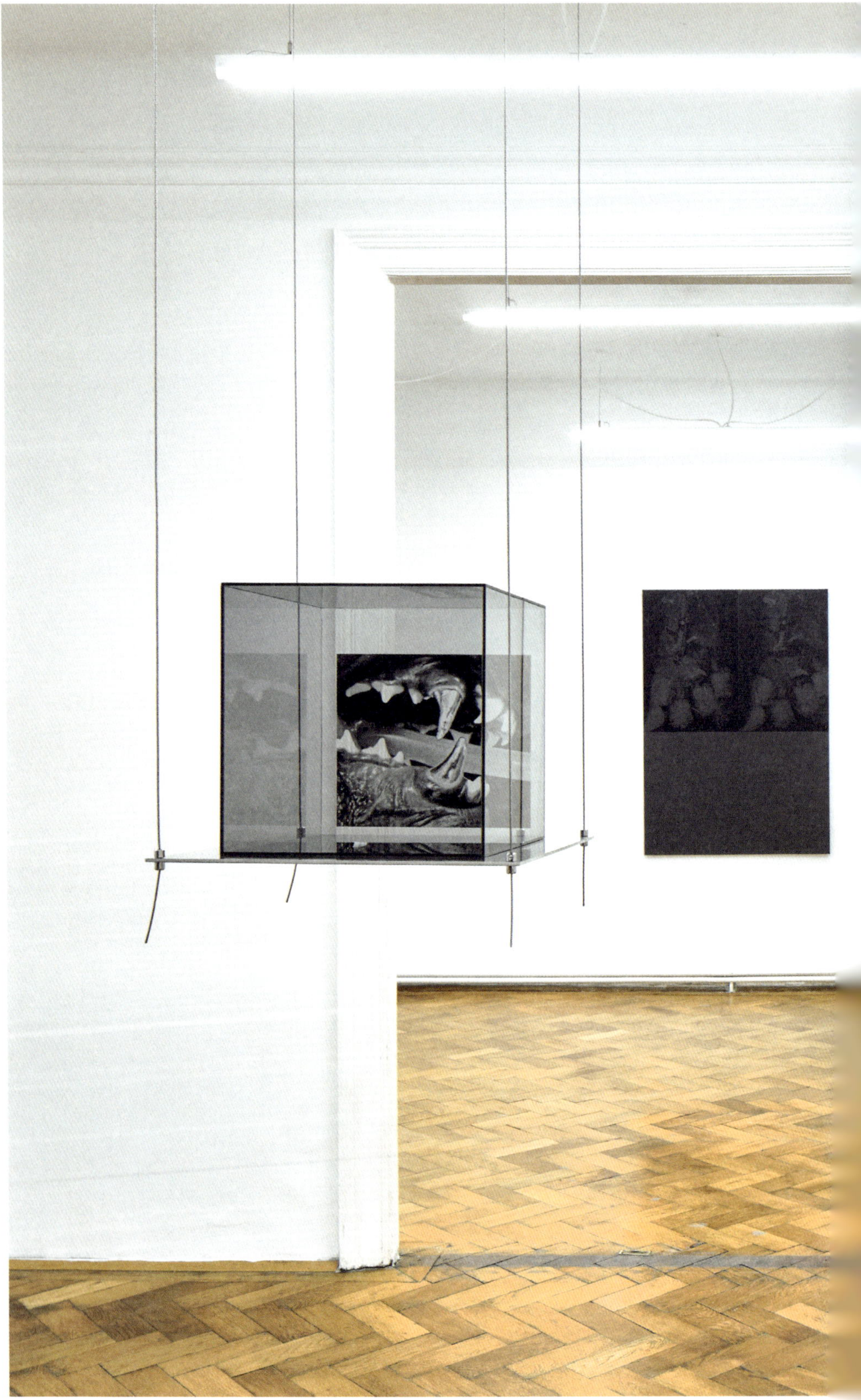

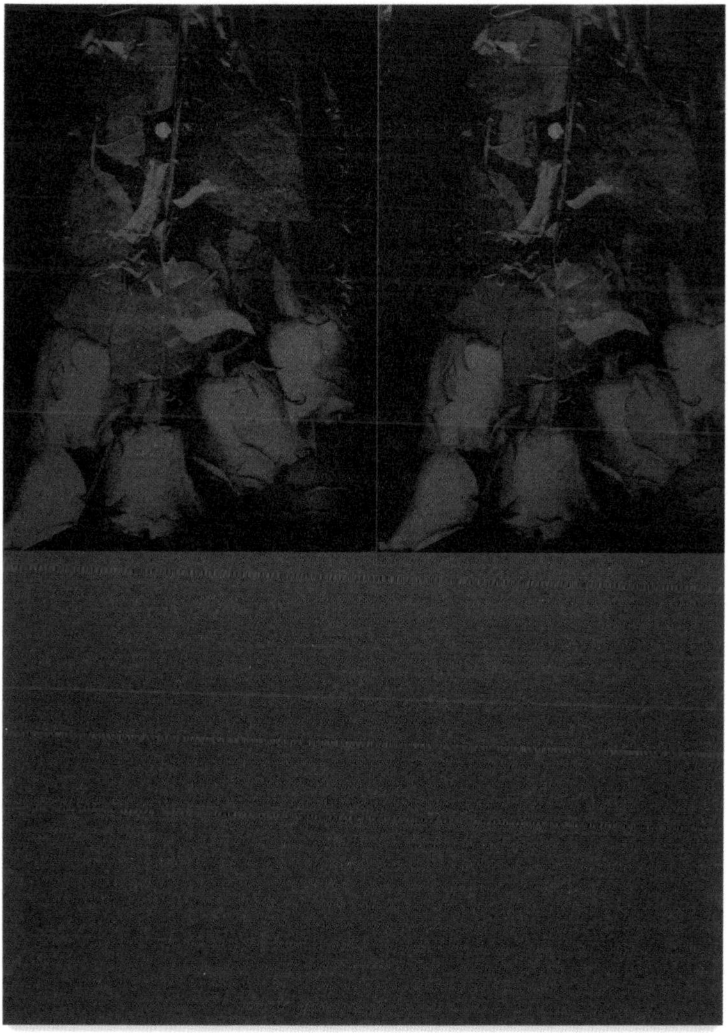

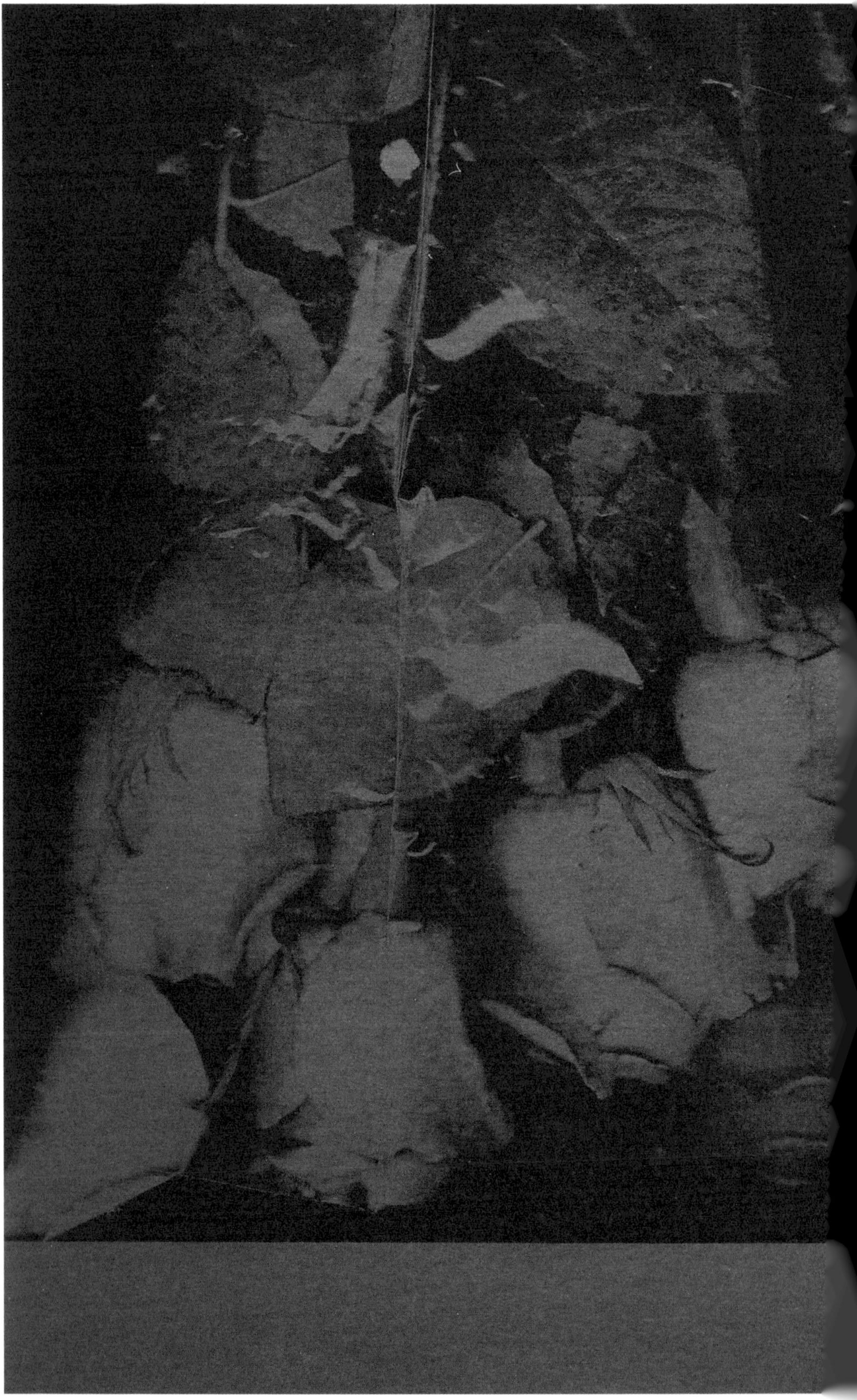

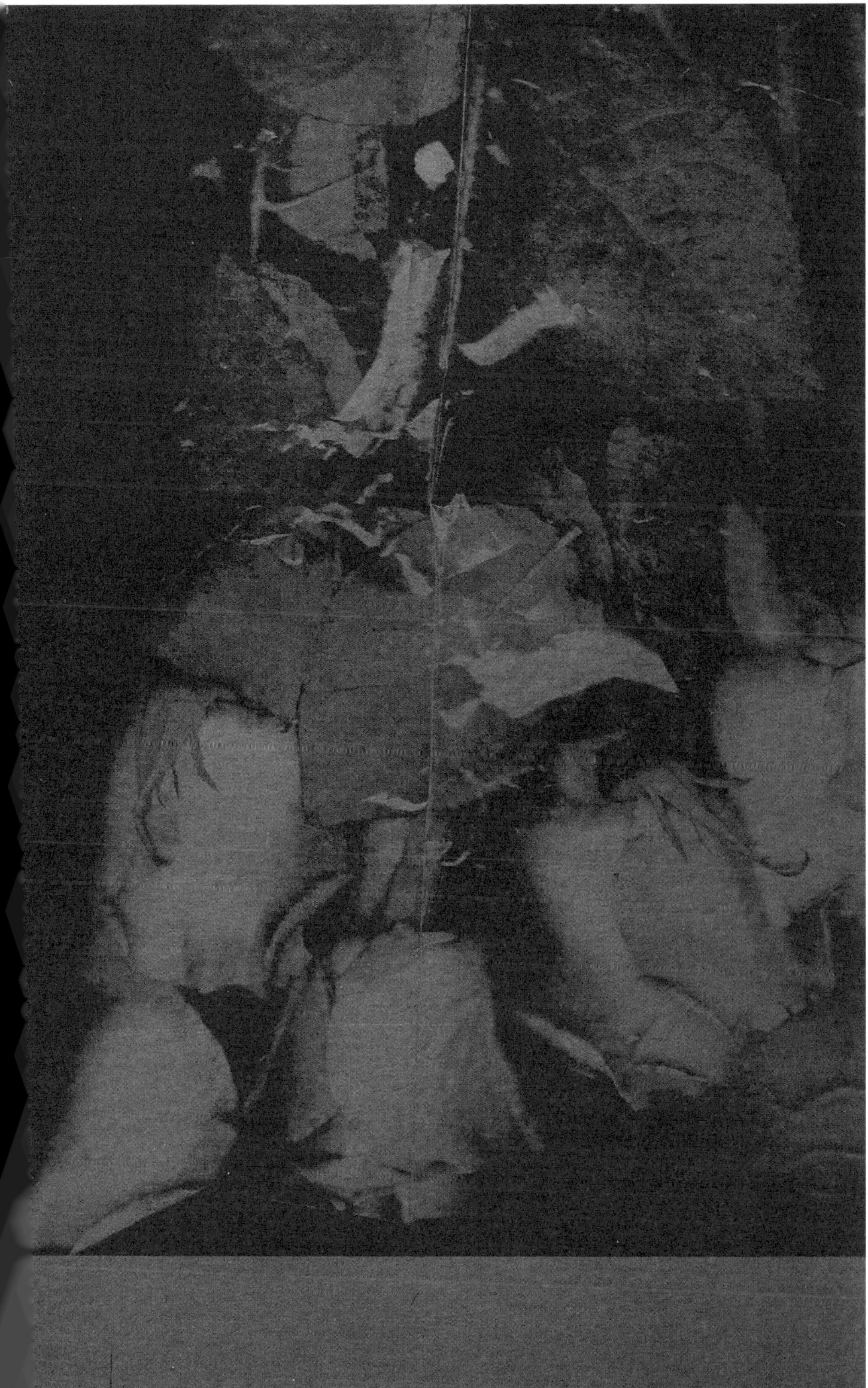

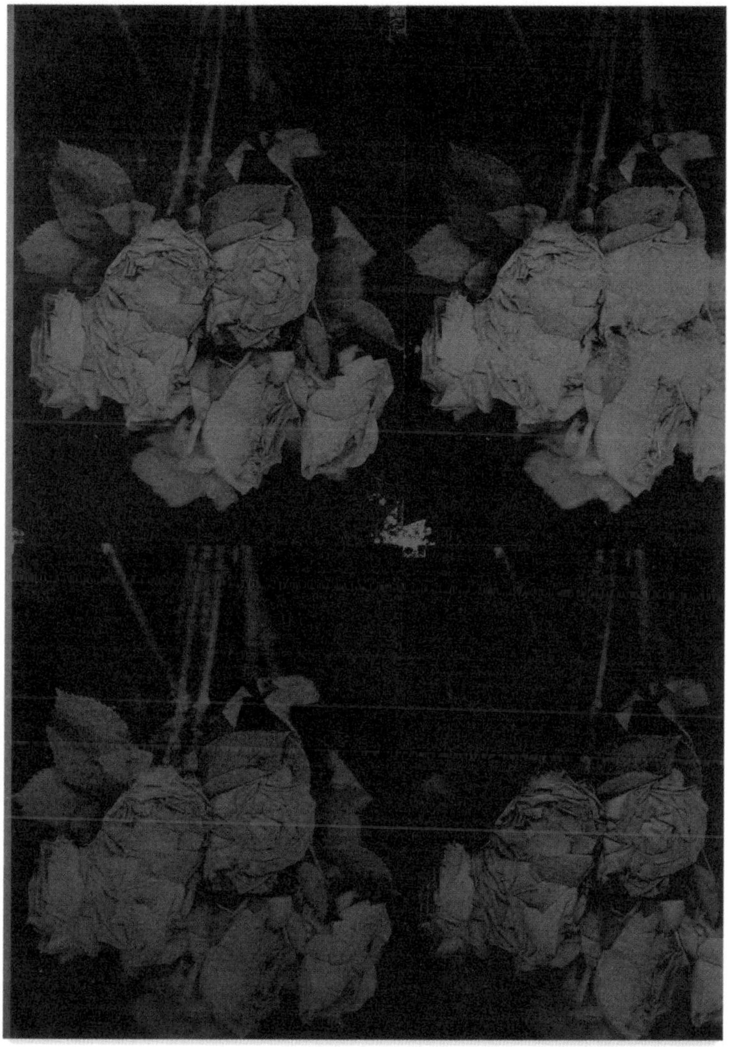

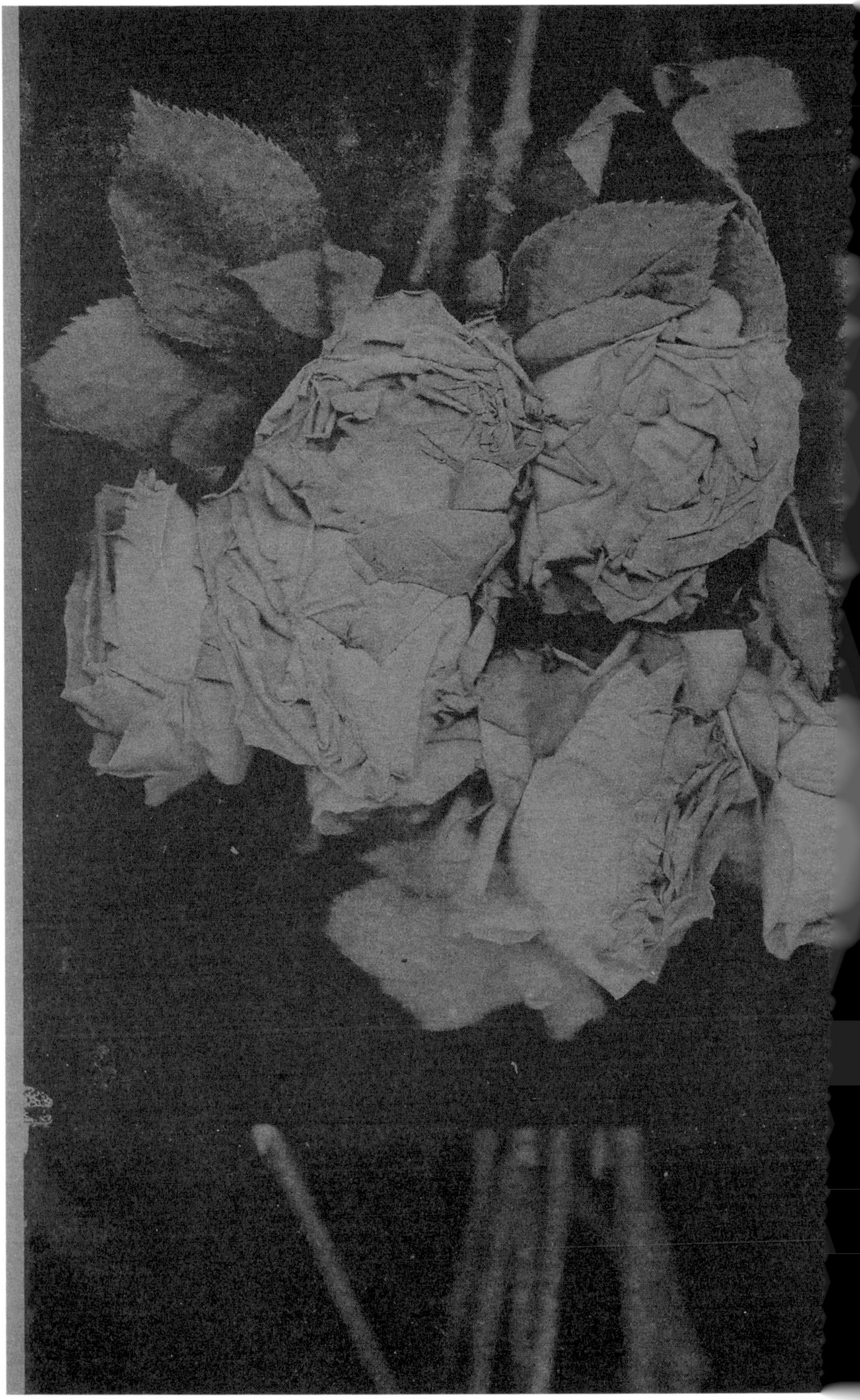

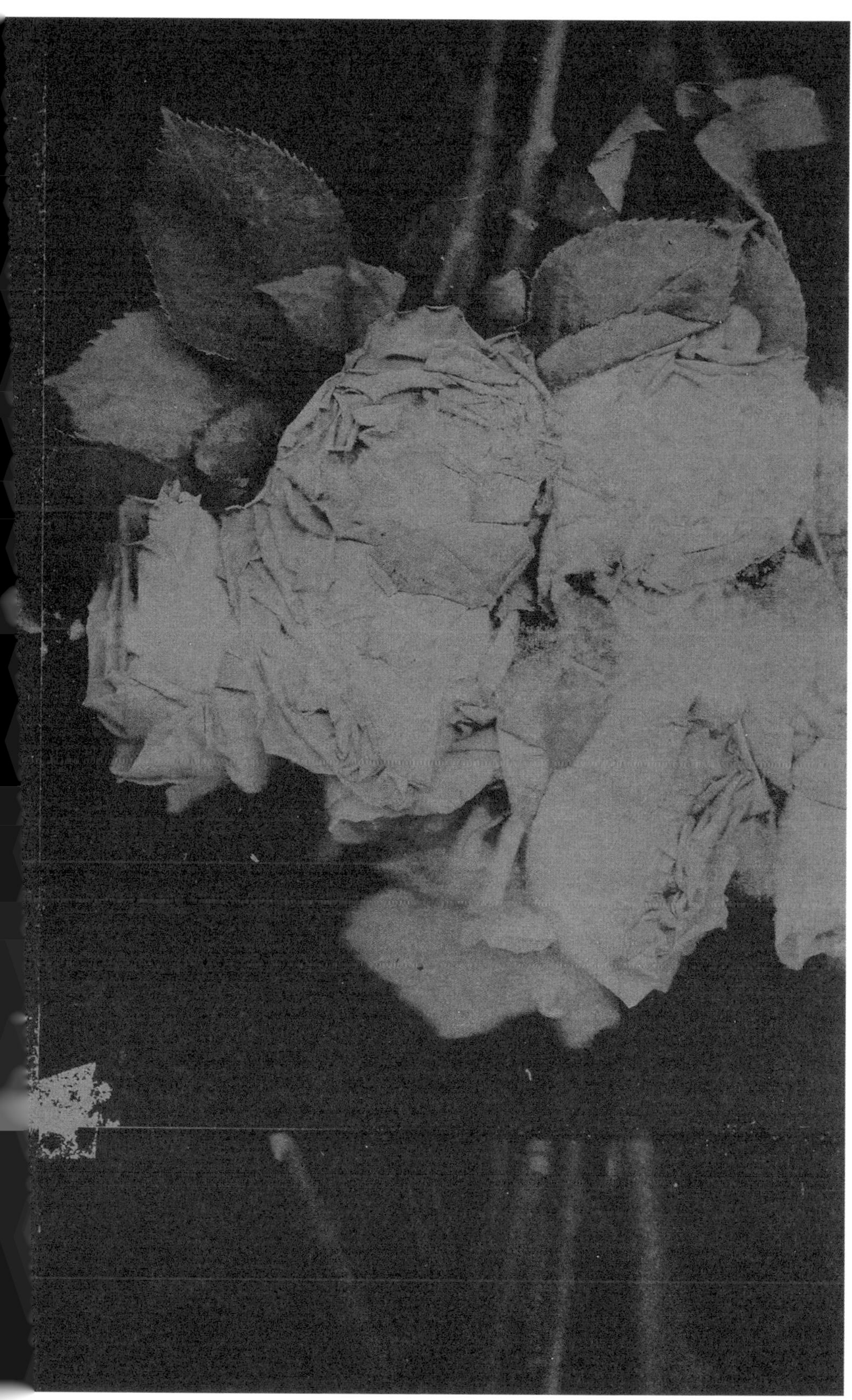

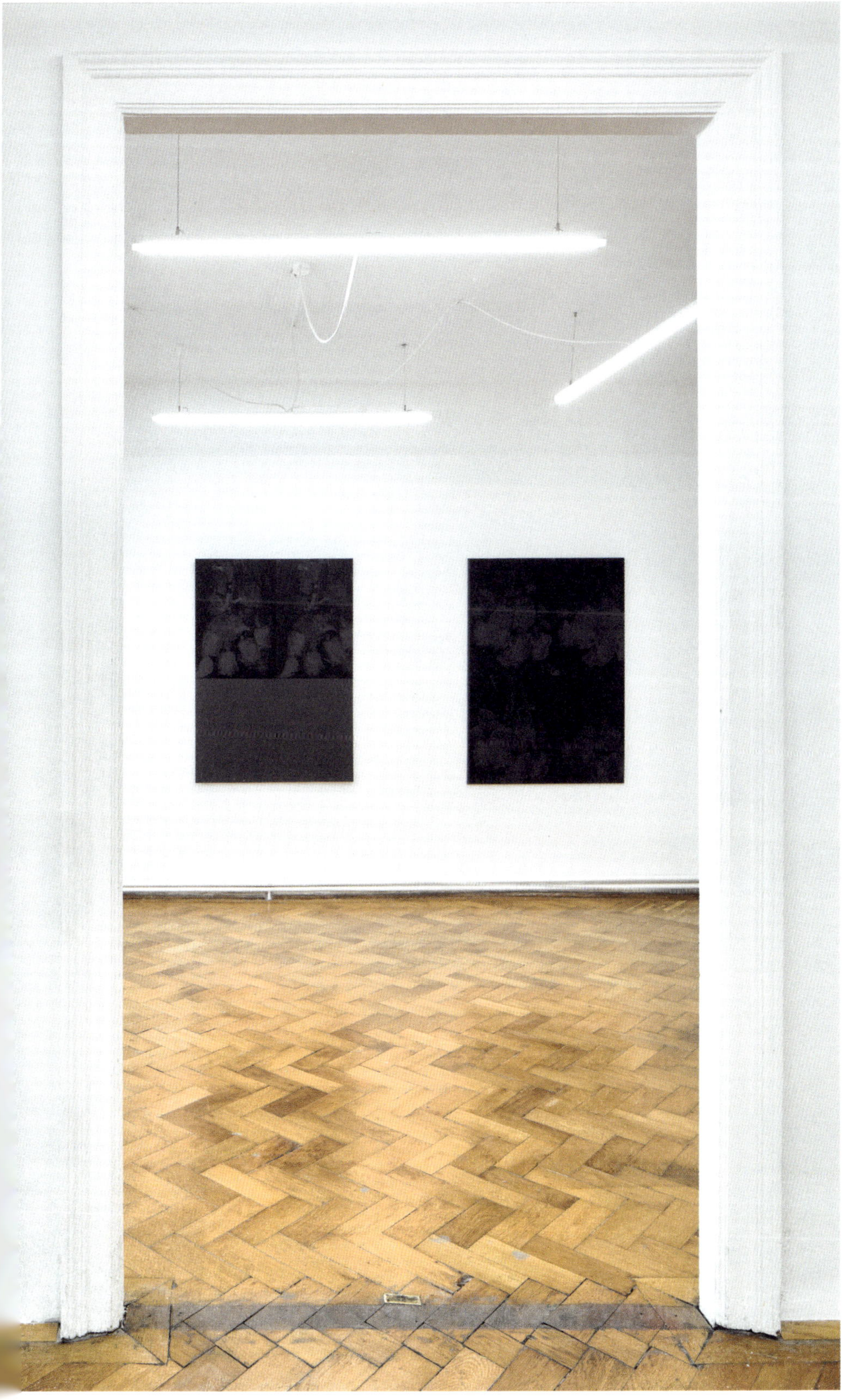

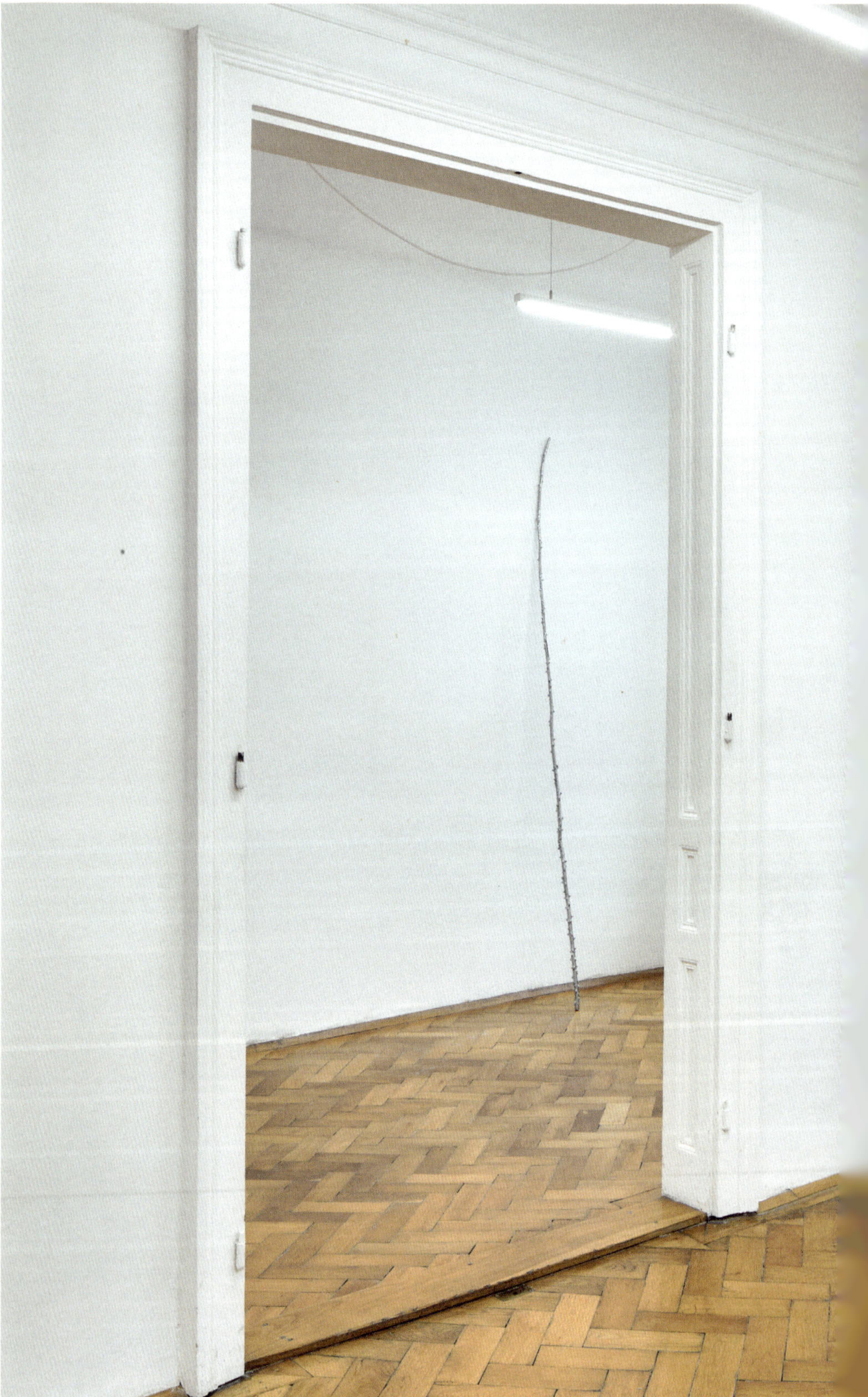

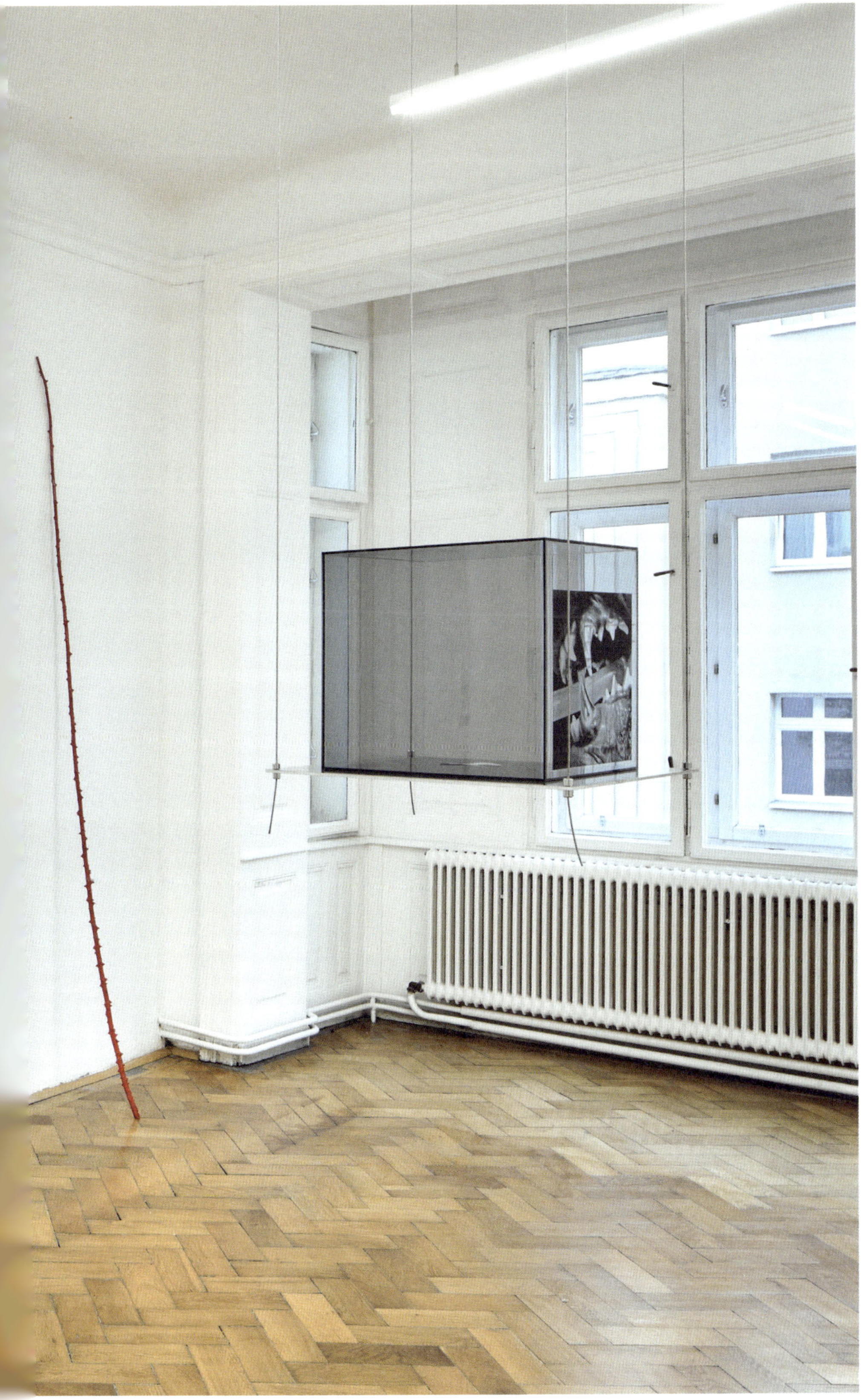

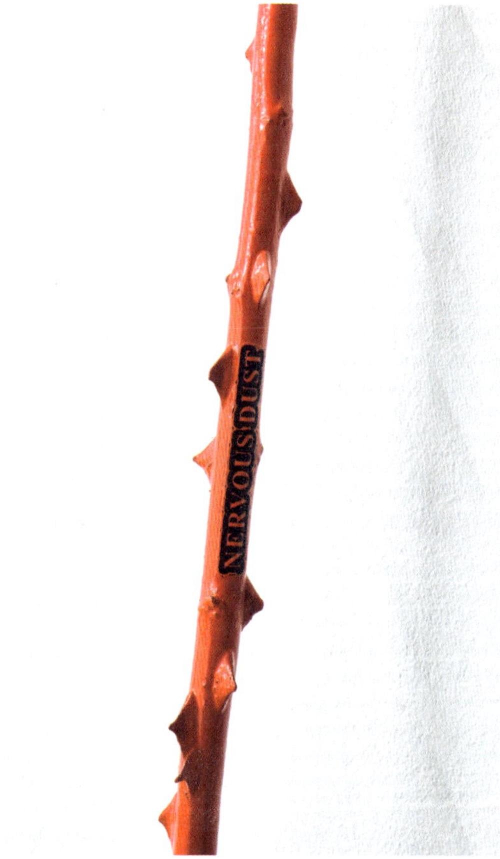
NERVOUS DUST

untitled (...)

Three thorny vines. Isolated. In different colors. In its clarity, the form is disconcertingly natural and unnaturally disconcerting; it exerts a strange power of attraction. Red. Chrome. The coatings on these thorny branches are as banal as they are striking. Bronze... just like the alloy from which they are cast. The material is as archaic as it is precious. Covered with individual stickers, the branches indicate a deliberate human intervention and yet defy straightforward categorization. What is it that makes these thorns seem so familiar, despite their contradictory form?

Thorns are part of a natural defense mechanism. Plants like the rose bush bear thorns to ward off threats and survive in their environment. Often, those who are able to break through these defenses are not a threat, but rather a part of a natural cycle that ensures survival. Beyond that, it's necessary to stay away from the repellent thorns. Thorny branches are therefore initially a deterrent; they pose a symbolic danger, they warn against themselves...

(soft sorrow)

The thorny branch leans against the wall, simultaneously solitary and iconic. With its larger-than-life size, it seems as fragile as it is menacing and, standing there, abandoned, breaks with our viewing habits. As a bronze cast, the branch is unsettling, unnatural, cut off from the world, perhaps even alien. There is a sticker on it—*soft sorrow*—which has a condemnatory effect similar to the thorny branch itself. What kind of sorrow is being lamented here? And is it not the soft sorrow that we can indulge ourselves in, melancholically—which is always there and yet not entirely perceptible?

Established in Christian iconography as an instrument of suffering, the branch of thorns is, at least in those societies that have been shaped by the Christian faith, charged with meaning: sin, suffering, or (self-)punishment. There are biblical images of horror that are united in the form of the branch of thorns. But above all, bound as a crown, it is associated with the endurance of pain. At the same time, the thorny branch of a rose bush is romanticized in the world of fairy tales and myths, where it appears as an insurmountable obstacle that can only be conquered through gallantry, or as a symbol of virtue and eternal life. And although the rose is symbolic of beauty and love and generally enjoys a reputation as the most romantic of flowers (and can therefore also be exploited for capitalist purposes), these positive connotations are reserved for the blossom and not the stem of the rose bush. It is the same in Greek mythology, in which the red rose is attributed to Aphrodite, the goddess of beauty and love, while the thorns represent her inner pain. But perhaps love and suffering are direct counterparts?

Whose sorrow is being described here? The everyday nature of the sticker reflects a reassuring normality, a comprehensibility that draws reference to our (own) emotional world—and which, contrary to the thorny defense that appears dangerous and impenetrable from the outside, if not even isolating, nevertheless indicates that gentle pain and soft sorrow are as personal as they are relatable, both normal and exceptional in equal measure. And which, besides all that, may also be worth protecting?

(nervous dust)

Elusive and slick, almost erotic, everything seems to drop like drew off the radiant red of the thorny branch. The color, which symbolizes strength and power, imbues the branch with an unattainable aura. The bold, industrial coloring is jarring in its interplay with the natural form, and yet makes it appear complete.

The cast under the vibrant red is created in a painstaking process, the result of which remains uncertain until the very end. During direct casting, the branch disintegrates under extreme heat over a period of hours (a relatively short time frame for the disappearance and dissolution into nothingness), leaving only the negative form inside of a shell. The form-giving element is lost; a hollow body is created, which is filled with bronze. The process cannot be repeated, because the (lost) model no longer exists.

One conclusion suggests itself: the process is an allegory for the transience of the tangible and organic, as well as for the endurance of the unnatural form(s) that can be taken from the model. In this sense, it is also an allusion to the fading-away of living bodies and what remains, often in the form of tales and devotion. Taken from life and yet at times far removed from it? Perhaps precisely because ephemeral things are being taken here and preserved for eternity. How is it decided which forms are carried into the future with their stories still attached? And which ones are left out?

nervous dust… like dust that's carelessly swept into a corner and yet stirred up again and again, the stickers on the thorny branches transport stories into the here and now. In just a few words, they tell of what's happening in the present, without waiting for the future. Stories that don't accept an "after," that are immediate (and relatable), and yet are told by only a few. Stories that do not remain silent in the face of seclusion, that speak of sorrow and pain, that demand closeness and desire affection. Those whose narratives deal with vulnerability and the possibility of admitting it. These are stories that make reflection possible; they are about disappearing, being held onto, and staying.

(cursed)

The chrome coating encases the thorny branch cast in bronze. The dullness of the bronze dissolves, and the shiny metal of the branch elevates it above its surroundings. It not only looks precious: it is. The reflective surface leaves no doubt as to its value; the defensive posture of the thorns gleams in its metallic luster. As already described, defense also means protection: thorns represent an invincible shell around a vulnerable core.

According to many traditions and stories, anyone who is cursed is considered to be defenseless against it, since in many cases, those who have been cursed know neither by whom nor why. Curses are difficult to break, because they strike at the very core that needs to be protected. *cursed* therefore describes a state that is uncontrollable, difficult to influence, and often beyond one's own scope of action. At the same time, there is something dark and supernatural about the curse that cannot be categorized in worldly terms. Those who seem to be cursed often move to the margins of society, appear solitary, become isolated. In the experience of feeling cut off from society, it is possible to draw strength, develop resilience, and reposition oneself.

Perhaps it is the ordinariness of a sticker that can bring comfort—an ordinariness that doesn't judge, but is accessible and comprehensible. This comprehensibility can be both sublime and threatening, natural and disturbing, tangible and slippery. And it makes no distinction between Red. Chrome. Bronze.

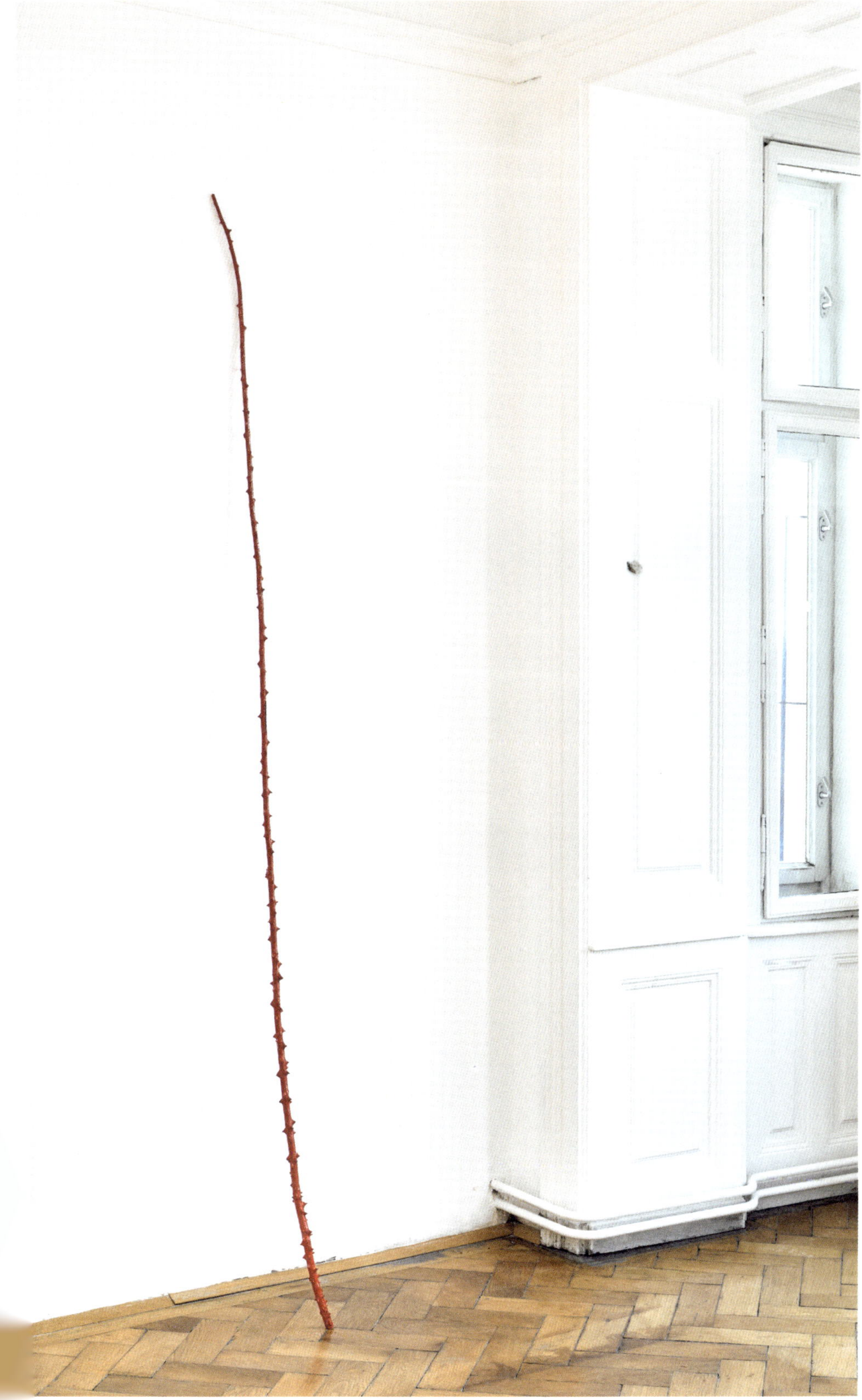

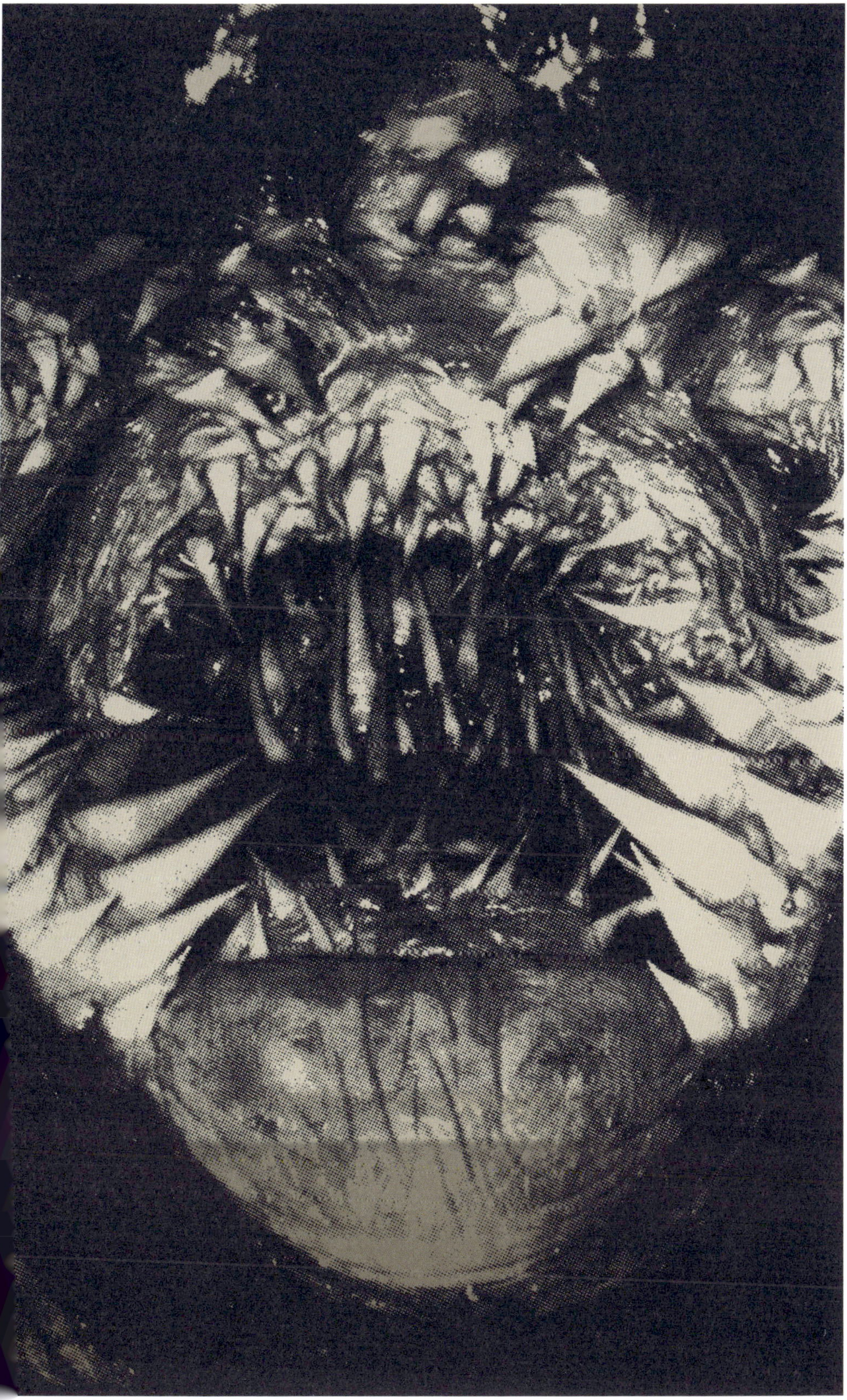

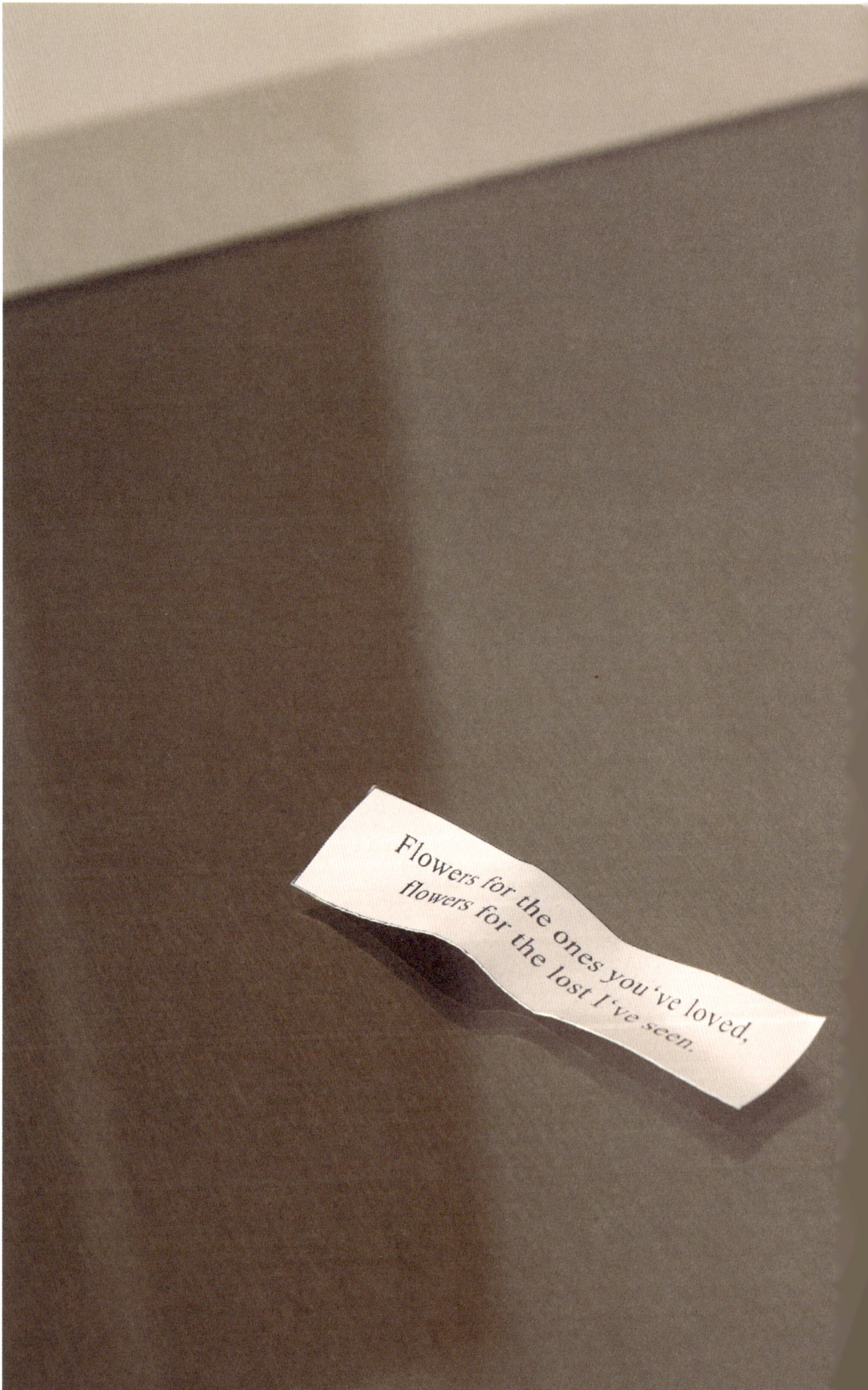
Flowers for the ones you've loved,
flowers for the lost I've seen.

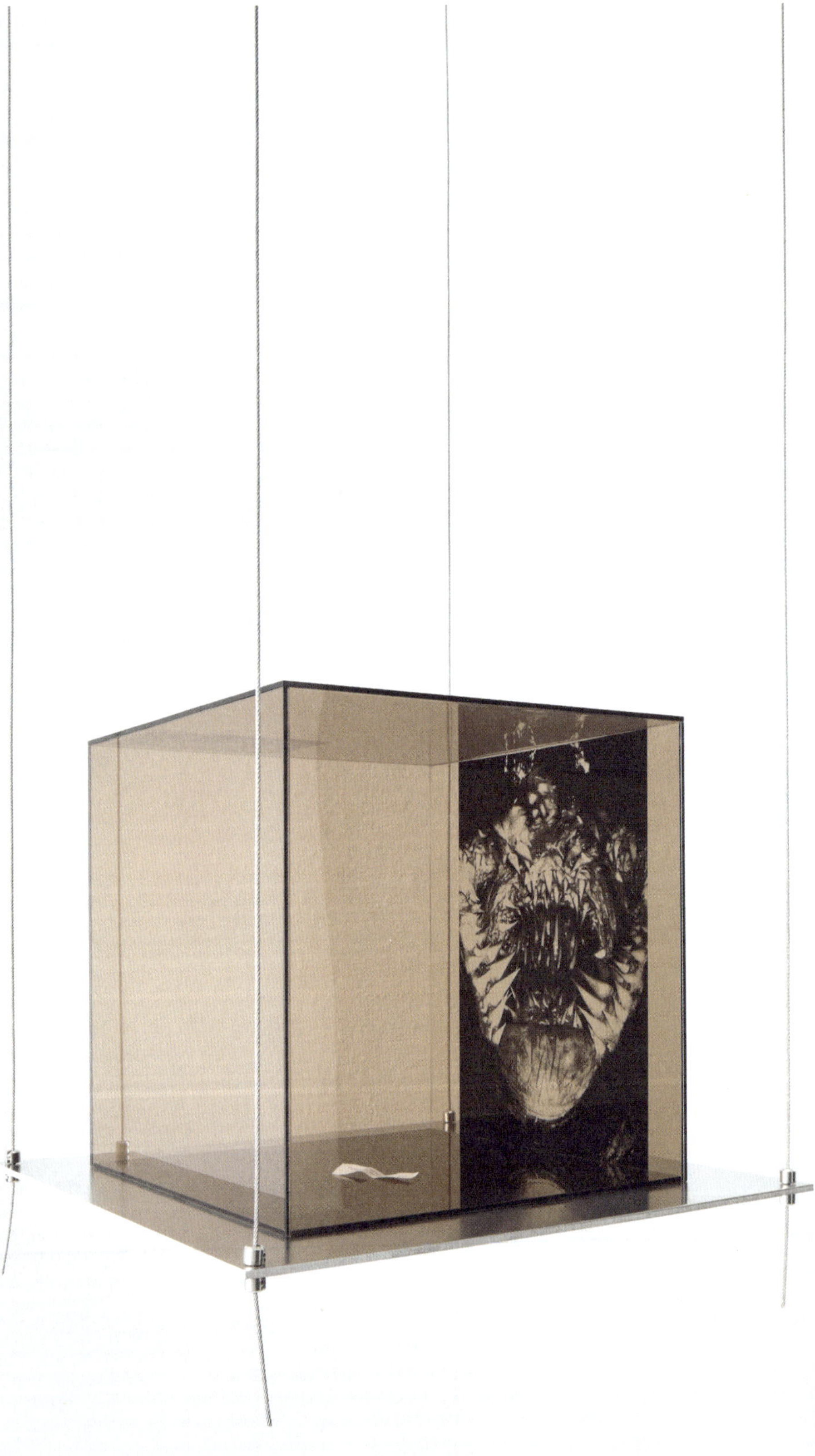

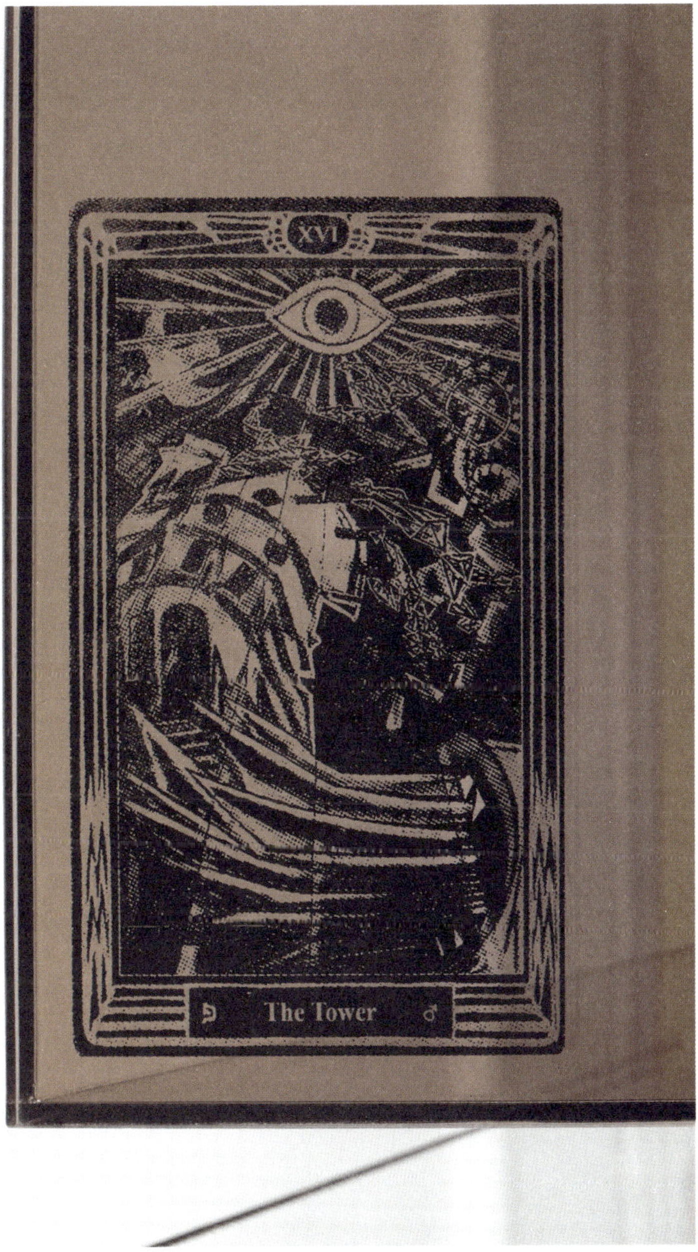
XVI
The Tower

I swallowed the sun,
yet no rays can replace
the warmth of your shadow.

In my dreams,
each night,
I am alone.

My hand reaches for a flower with no name,
finding its glow,
shy from the light.

Farewell always hurts
until the peacock's cry
draws closer to the edge of the urn.

This night is lit by thorns,
unwrapping my eye
like a dust fruit amidst the axis of the stars,
to see—

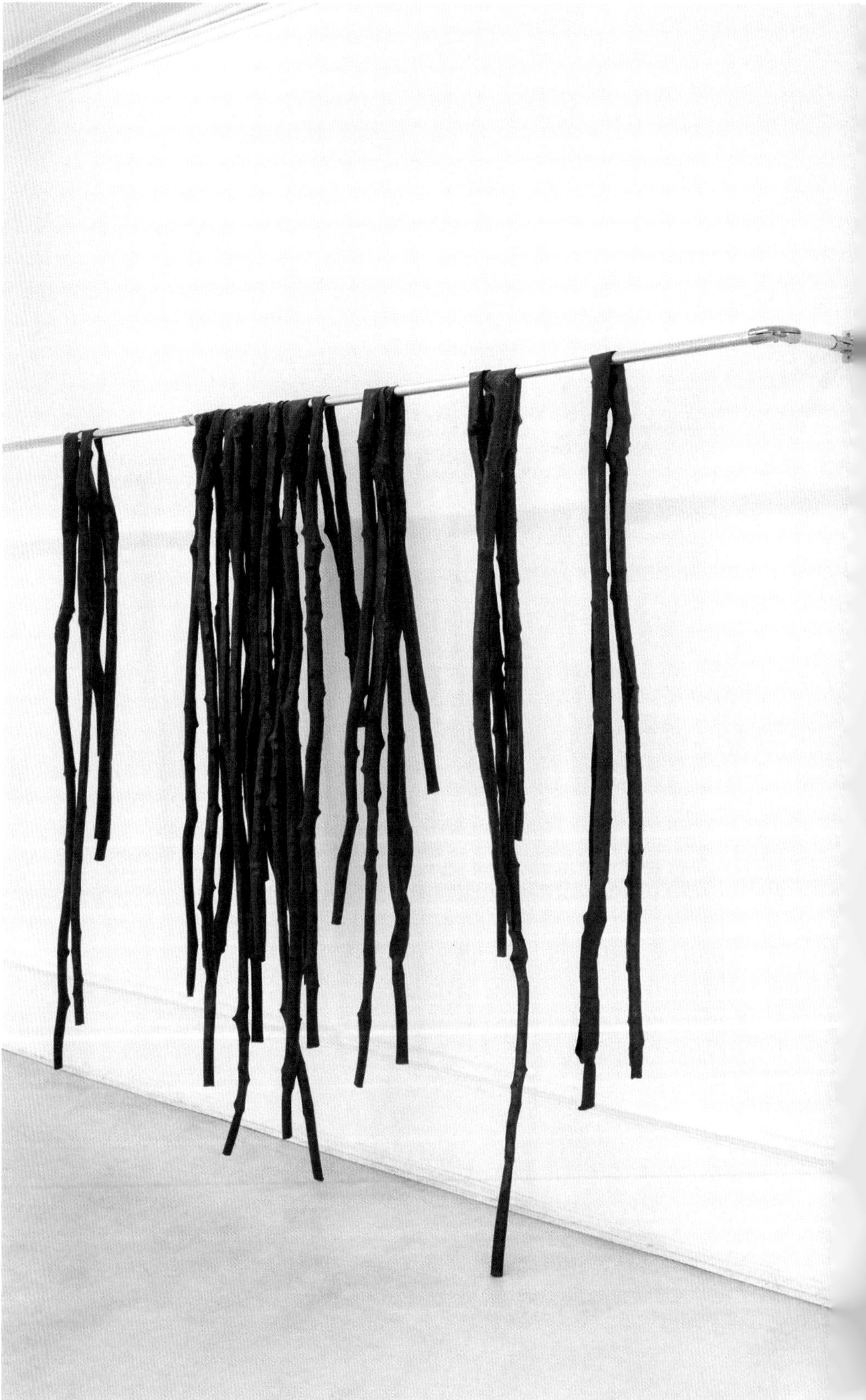

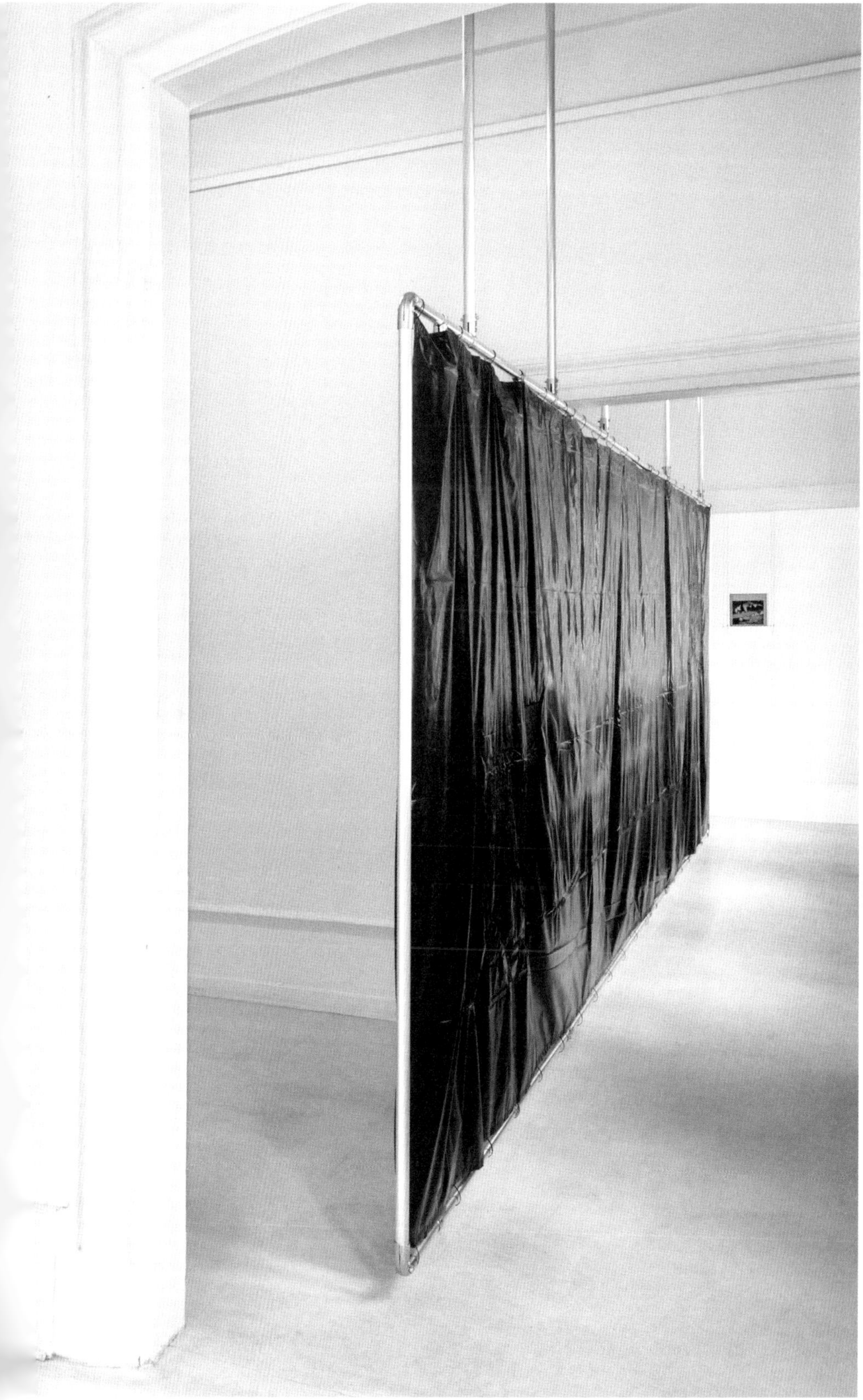

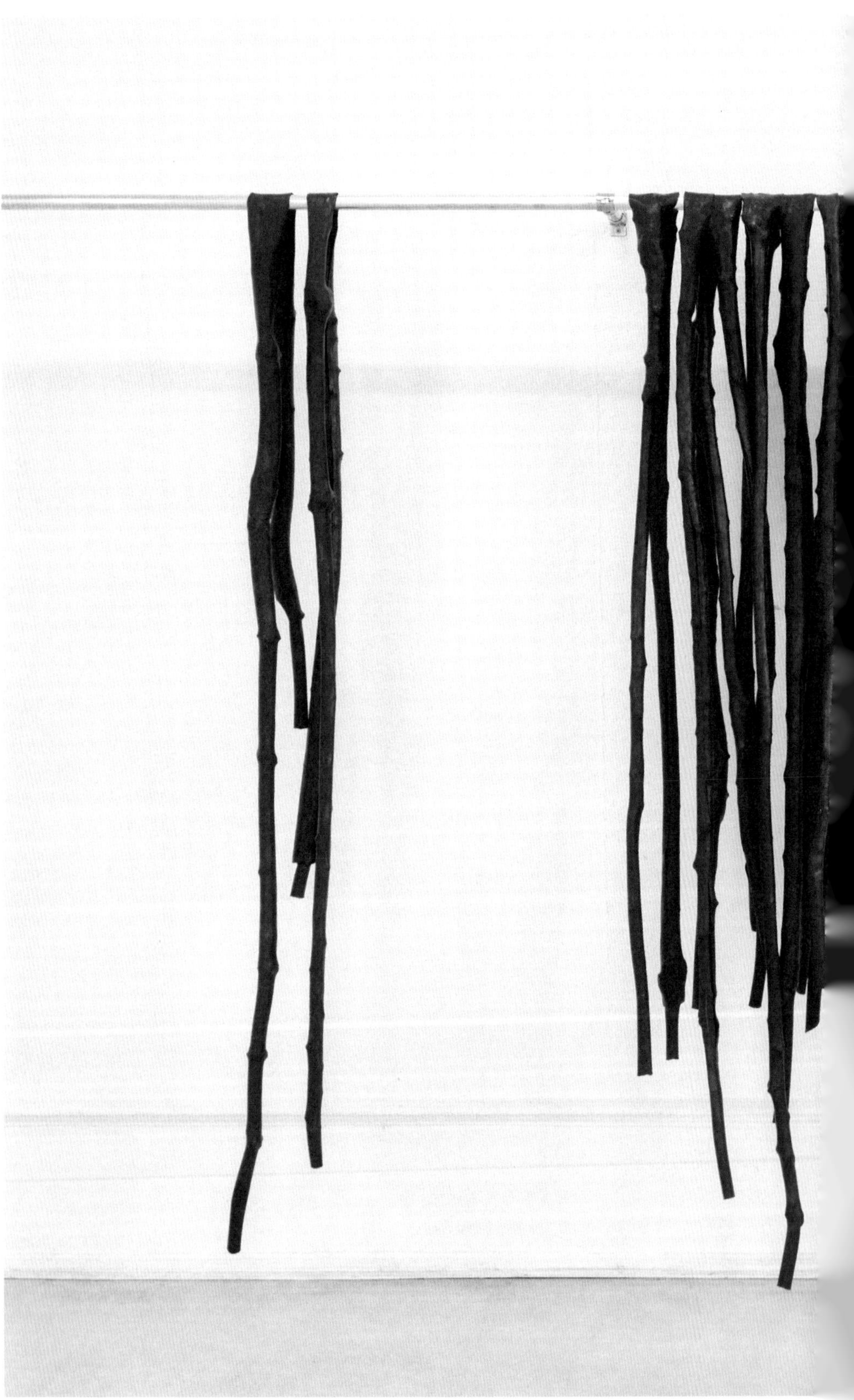

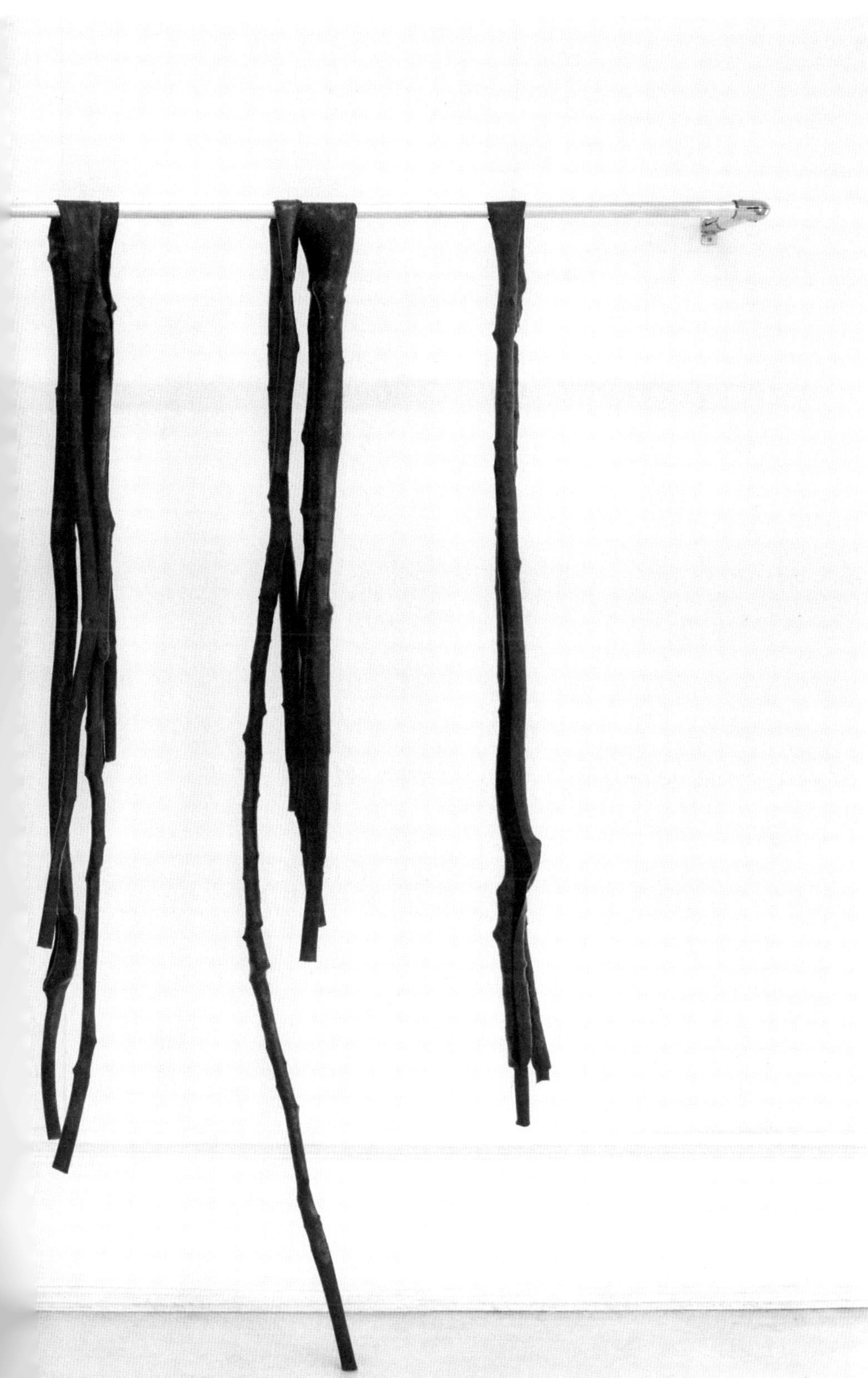

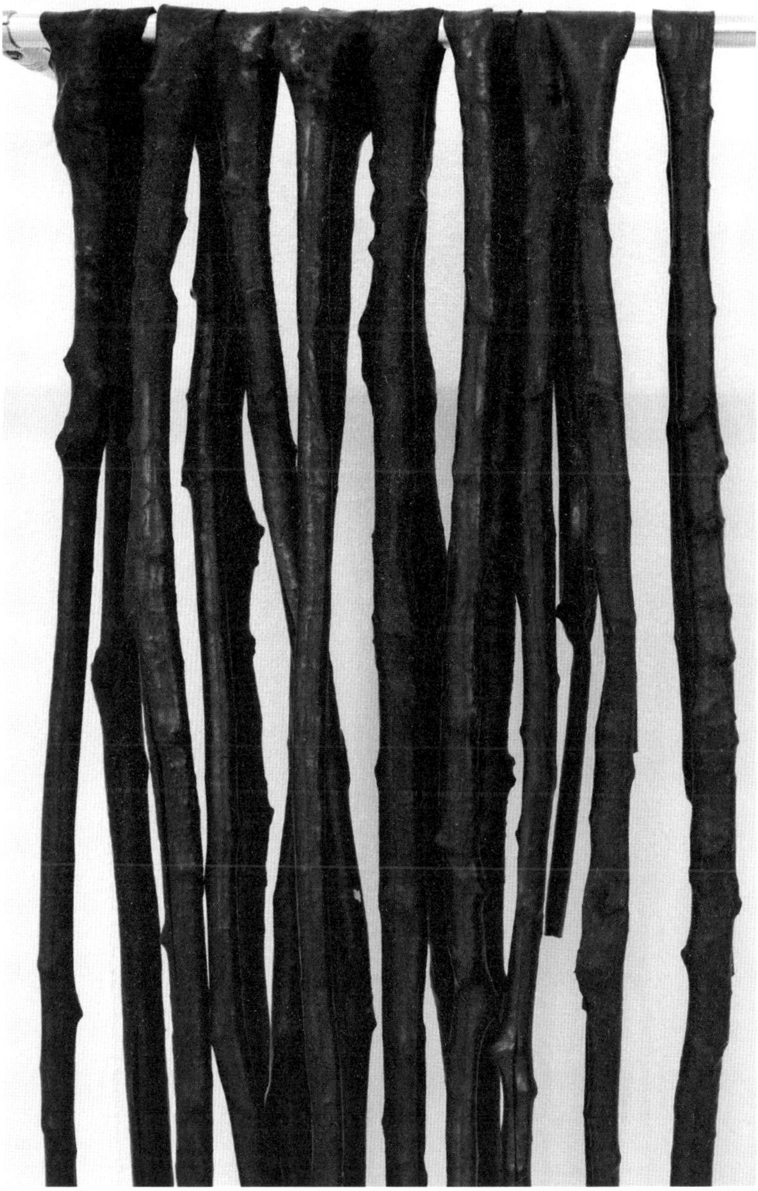

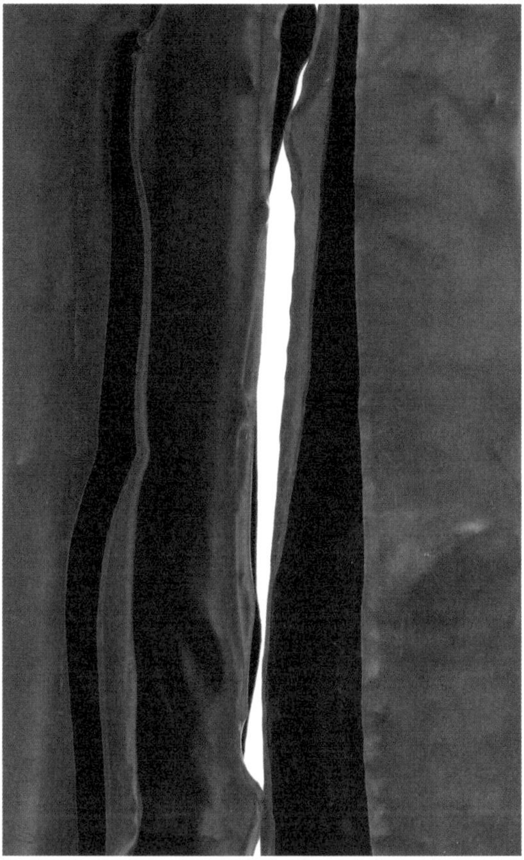

"Death is the most uninteresting thing in my work," Martin told me during our Zoom chat.

The following chapters, "Hermeticism," "Sad Songs," and "Speechlessness," are attempts to apply some sort of systematic approach to the element of language within his practice. In contrast to any precise scholarly analysis, this text uses the chapters to delve into other topics, pieces of art, and personal associations.

Hermeticism

The color black might not only absorb light, but also language.

In his solo exhibition *Nervous Dust* (2022) Martin presented malleable, synthetic tubes, hanging limp from an aluminum rod. *Untitled (After All 1+2)* (2019/2020) is made with shrink tubing, a thermoplastic material that contracts in size when heated and is commonly used for electrical insulation and to protect broken wires and cables. Martin used shrink tubing to mold natural birch branches, resulting in an appearance and feeling of lifeless, hollow shells or skins. They are precisely dissected, containing the remaining particles of the bark that once belonged to a living tree.

With the idea of shrink tubing, or a process of wrapping and enclosing an object very firmly, I want to write about the hermetic nature of Martin's artistic language. The word "hermetic" in its very practical sense means that something—for example, an object—is isolated from outside influence, tightly sealed off from the external environment. Of course, the works are not literally sealed off from their surroundings, but they bear a certain sense of inwardness. His architectural constructions are sourced from plastic packaging that used to contain burial soil. These constructions, which could be identified as displays, build temporal compartments within the spaces of their presentation, allowing for an intimate experience. The black foil is reminiscent of the ground which seals off the dead from the living. Even here, the color evokes a sense of cold; it is one that absorbs most, if not all light. It converts incoming energy into heat.

They tried to bury me, they didn't realize I was a seed.
Sinéad O'Connor

There are a number of works in Martin's oeuvre that, in contrast to the pieces that absorb light, reflect it and allude to a less technical idea around the adjective hermetic and are affiliated with the meaning of its noun Hermeticism, or Hermetism.

This philosophical and spiritual tradition dates back to ancient Egypt and is attributed to the mythical figure Hermes Trismegistus. The core belief of Hermeticism is that there is a hidden, sacred knowledge that can reveal the nature of reality and the divine. This knowledge, often referred to as the *Corpus Hermeticum* (Hermetic corpus), comprises a series of writings and teachings exploring various metaphysical and mystical concepts. Hermeticism emphasizes the principle of correspondence, which states that there are connections and similarities between the microcosm (human) and the macrocosm (universe). As above, so below—the patterns found in the heavens are reflected in earthly life. Alchemy is an integral part of Hermeticism, aiming to transmute base metals into gold as an allegory for spiritual transformation and self-empowerment. The process of alchemy involves purification, dissolution, and integration of the self. Hermeticism had a significant influence on the development of Western esotericism, occultism, and some elements of Renaissance thought. Its ideas have been incorporated into various mystical traditions and secret societies throughout history. The development of individual belief systems creates codes that point to something beyond the physical world. These codes remain present, as they debunk ahistorical thinking and a mythic construction of the self against all odds.

In a permanent search for meaning, the artist James Lee Byars extracted mythological references that he adapted to his discourse. Using specific materials, he structured cryptic concepts of perfection, questioning the illegibility of a world whose materialism seems to have expelled any consideration of the sacred. His work *The Rose Table of Perfect* (1989) is a 100-cm diameter spherical sculpture made of 3,333 fresh red roses that slowly wither during the exhibition period.

In the summer of 1966, twenty-three years earlier, the artist Paul Thek, with his lover, photographer Peter Hujar, visited the Capuchin catacombs of Palermo, where he was deeply struck by the "8000 corpses used to decorate a room, like flowers." He responded to this moment using the Catholic tradition of relics. In his *Technological Reliquaries* (1966), acrylic glass boxes are filled with wax replicas of bodies.

In Martin's series of translucent plexiglass boxes bearing silkscreen prints of rather disturbing images, as well as Thot Tarot cards by Aleister Crowley, the artist's interest in systems of beliefs, coded practices, and enigmatic rituals becomes most evident. Thought of as contemporary reliquaries, these works evoke ancient archetypes of decorated containers or shrines made from precious materials, containing artifacts associated with saints that provide visual access to a spiritual world. The boxes appear to have been brought back from a bleak future in which human and animal life has been reduced to nothing more than the lost debris of a cataclysmic past.

In *Untitled (The Moon)* (2022), we sense the mouth of a dog with a respiration tube between its teeth–a brutal preparation for the thought of losing a loved one—paired with the tarot card The Moon. The card features Anubis, the jackal-headed Egyptian god of the underworld, who guides the dead through the afterlife. The box contains a paper with the sentence, "In my dreams you don't want the best for me."

In *Untitled (The Tower)* (2022), we encounter prints of a leatherback turtle's mouth and the tarot card The Tower. The card features a collapsing tower with human figures falling into a chasm. In the right corner of the card is a gigantic pair of fire-breathing jaws at the root of the structure. *Untitled (The Tower)* carries a small piece of paper with the words, "Flowers for the ones you've loved, flowers for the lost I've seen." The thought of a turtle mouth seems rather harmless, but the mouth of this particular species entirely lacks teeth; instead it has what are known as "papillae" or "spines." The papillae are sharp, backward-pointing projections lining the leatherback's throat and gullet.

Martin's boxes represent a semiotic system of nonverbal and visual messages, implicated in activating memories due to communicative connection to the missing and hidden. They seem meaningful, but are also deceptive, capable of changing their meanings dynamically, depending on the context they are situated in. They can be envisioned as psychological signifiers that have been deprived of their original context. Words appear not only directly on the objects, but since the latter are deeply informed by an interest in and knowledge of symbols and metaphors, they themselves also function like words in a poem, as they are vessels beyond their ostensible meaning. They offer aesthetic and rhythmic compositions that point to second, third, and fourth layers of meaning.

Sad Songs

When Martin and I talked about the little sheets of papers in the boxes, he mentioned *Sad Songs*, tracks of music that he would listen to when he was a teenager or adult. Fascinated by the music of CocoRosie and ANOHNI, he would be very attentive and receptive to the lyrics, but sometimes understand them slightly wrong.

This unintended interpretation of the texts reveals the great potential of language that is only communicated verbally. In *Orality and Literacy: The Technologizing of the Word* (1982), the media theorist Walter J. Ong explores the profound impact of communication technologies, specifically the shift from oral to written language, on human cognition, culture, and consciousness:

> *Fully literate persons can only with great difficulty imagine what a primary oral culture is like, that is, a culture with no knowledge whatsoever of writing or even of the possibility of writing. Try to imagine a culture where no one has ever 'looked up' anything. In a primary oral culture, the expression 'to look up something' is an empty phrase: it would have no conceivable meaning. Without writing, words as such have no visual presence, even when the objects they represent are visual. They are sounds. You might 'call' them back—'recall' them. But there is nowhere to 'look' for them. They have no focus and no trace (a visual metaphor, showing dependency on writing), not even a trajectory. They are occurrences.*

Let's recall these songs and think of them as occurrences.

In my early twenties, I discovered CocoRosie and ANOHNI. When I think about this time in my life, I remember how precious music was. It was a way to express one's own taste, it served as one of the many tools to distinguish oneself from others, it showed a certain sense of connoisseurship, an expertise in underground music. Going to the store and buying the CDs was like going to flea markets and finding unique treasures that nobody knew about, or only a very small circle of friends. Back then I was already intrigued by the significance of art in CocoRosie's practice. Sierra and Bianca Cassady would bring the tales of their naïve songs to life by dressing up as fairy-tale creatures, working with collages that they would project at the back of their concert stages. Even though their language and stage characters seem naïve, their performances were filled with erotic fantasies and feminist ideas. I felt very drawn to this escapist world and was fascinated by Bianca's soft masculine appearance.

I wasn't able to put words to this fascination, but it went beyond their music and art, and shook something within me that I didn't know existed.

Today I would call it a sort of queerness *avant la lettre.*

Thinking about ANOHNI today, the image on the cover of their album *I Am a Bird Now* (2005) pops up in my head: a portrait by Peter Hujar of Candy Darling, a Warhol superstar and transgender icon, on her deathbed. Peter Hujar (1934–1987) was an American photographer known for his evocative black-and-white portraits and documentary-style images. He gained prominence in the 1970s and 1980s, capturing the vibrant and diverse artistic and LGBTQIA+ communities in New York City during that era. Hujar's photography often explored themes of mortality, beauty, and the human condition, and he was deeply influenced by classical art and literature. His works continue to be celebrated for their raw emotional power and insightful portrayal of marginalized individuals and the changing urban landscape. Despite his untimely death from AIDS-related complications, Peter Hujar's legacy as a significant figure in the history of photography remains enduring and influential.

I learned more about Hujar while I was working on a substantial exhibition by David Wojnarowicz, an artist and activist who also died of complications due to AIDS. At the time, I was reading a book that became one of my favorites, *Gentrification of the Mind* (2012) by Sarah Schulman, an American writer and activist known for her contributions to queer literature and her advocacy of LGBTQIA+ rights.

The book investigates how the AIDS epidemic, real estate development, and political forces impacted New York City during the 1980s and 1990s, leading to the disappearance of diverse communities and LGBTQIA+ artistic subcultures, while advocating for the preservation of unique spaces and collective memory amidst urban homogenization. She particularly focuses on the East Village, which in the 1970s and 1980s was a vibrant and culturally rich neighborhood, known for its bohemian and countercultural scene. It was hit hard by the HIV/AIDS epidemic in the 1980s. The neighborhood became a focal point for the crisis, with a high number of HIV/AIDS-related illnesses and deaths. As the state refused to provide care for the sick and secluded them from society, many had to leave the city and move in with their family or friends to be taken care of and die. As a result, the demographic of the East Village changed. The neighborhood's once affordable rents and abandoned spaces became attractive to more affluent individuals and developers seeking to capitalize on its central location. The influx of wealthier residents brought changes to the area's demographics and culture, displacing many long-time residents and artists who could no longer afford to live there.

Speechlessness

Grief is a cruel kind of education. You learn how ungentle mourning can be, how full of anger. You learn how glib condolences can feel. You learn how much grief is about language, the failure of language and the grasping for language.
Chimamanda Ngozi Adichie, *Notes on Grief* (2021)

As much as I try to analyze Martin's works, to find words for how they work, I always reach a point of frustration. It seems to me that words bounce off the works. In *Against Interpretation* (1964), Susan Sontag advocates for an "erotics of art," where the primary focus is on experiencing and appreciating the sensory and emotional qualities of the artwork. She calls for a more direct, instinctive engagement with art that allows the audience to respond emotionally and intuitively.

The erotics of Martin's works may lie in their hermetic character. Rather than talking to me as a viewer, they seem to talk to each other, like a system or logic of references in which each object resides within a designated space of meaning. What seems to lie at the core of Martin's works is a refusal to be successfully read in one way—a resistance to interpretation. Maybe this is due to his ambivalent combinations of images, objects, and words. This fragmentary appearance is based on the effect of cutting out a segment or piece from a larger whole. The idea of something more comprehensive blurs the sharp line of precise definitions. These fragments never search for the confirmation of definitions, but are always concerned about the threat of their dissolution. They appear like eerie symptoms of absence or exclusion. That's why they refuse immediacy.

Despite their hermetic presence, they are carriers of softness and sensitivity, directing our thoughts to care and vulnerability. Martin's installations and sculptures result in psychic spaces, embedded with intimate memories and seemingly familiar connections. His works do not offer any rational solutions to the issues they deal with. Within these gripping contradictions, they recall personal mythologies. They are isolated vessels of their own capacities, creating a poetic realm, operating unrecognizably, whether they are inside or outside, permeating the individual drama of the self.

The taste of sorrow might be soft.

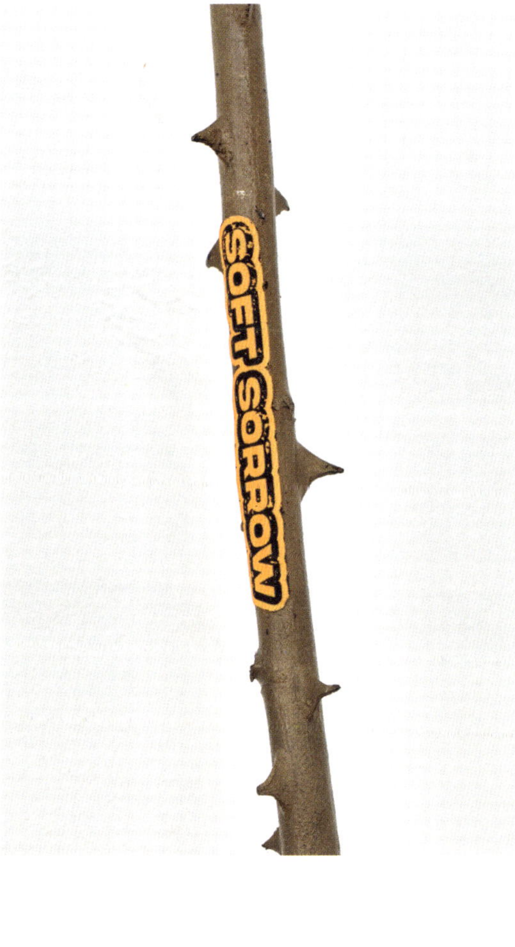
SOFT SORROW

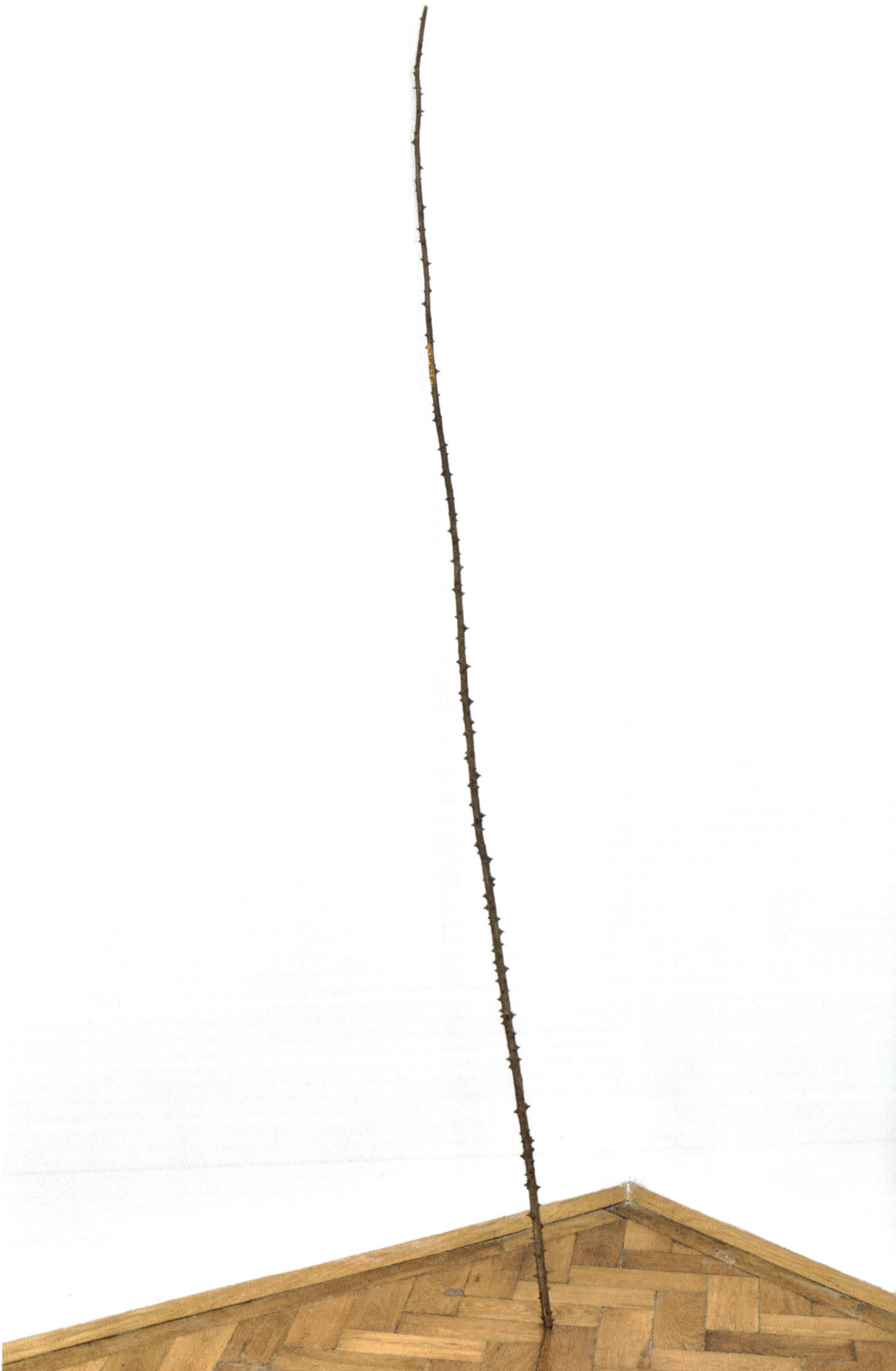

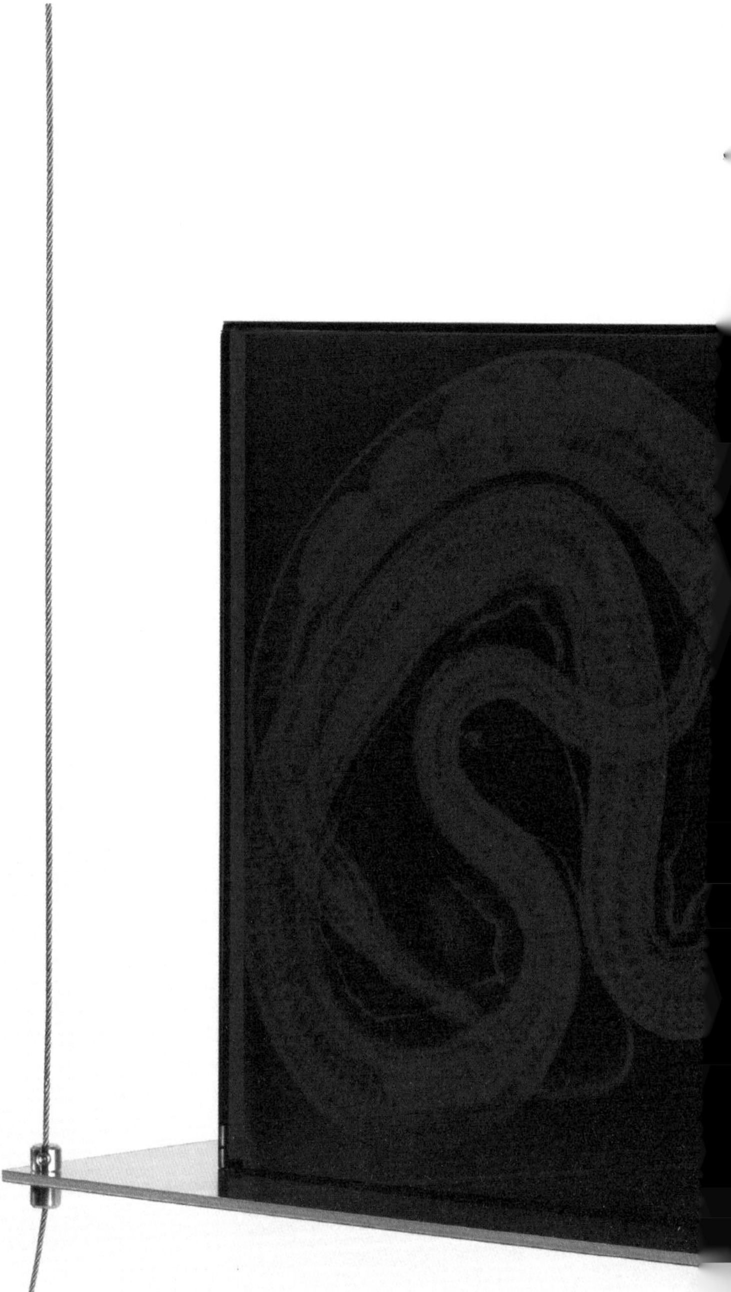

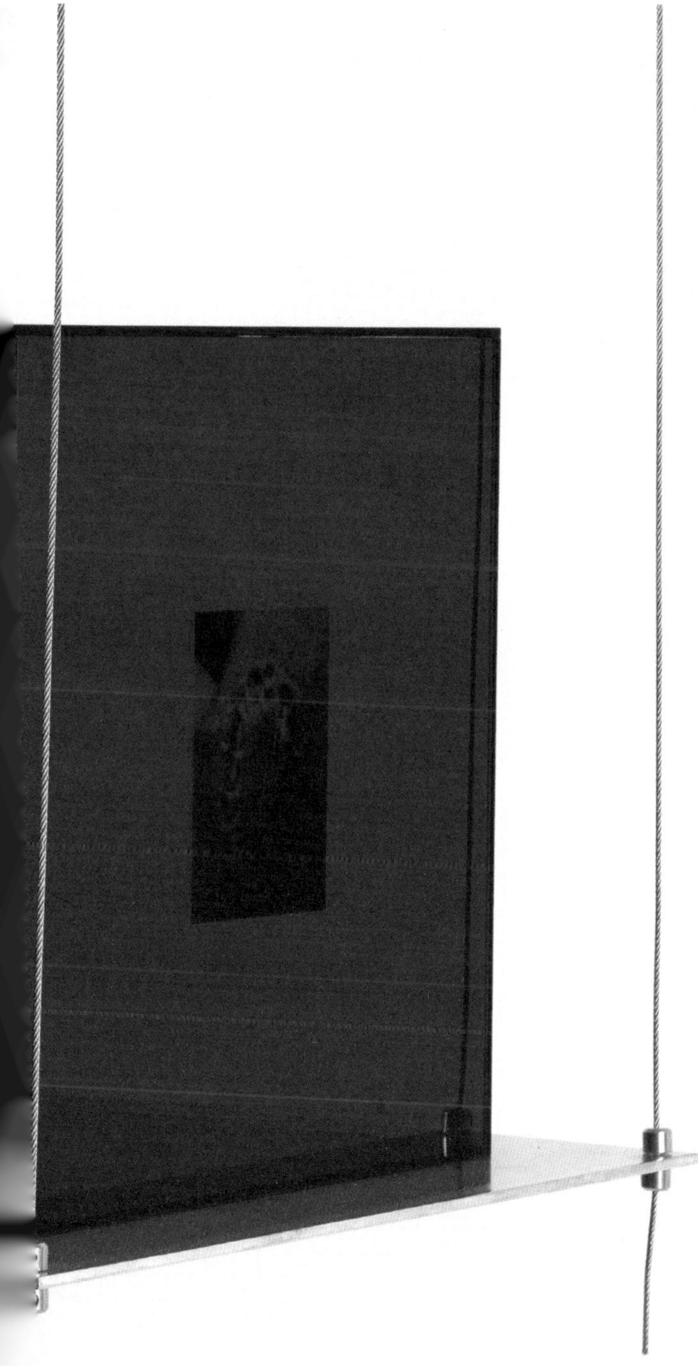

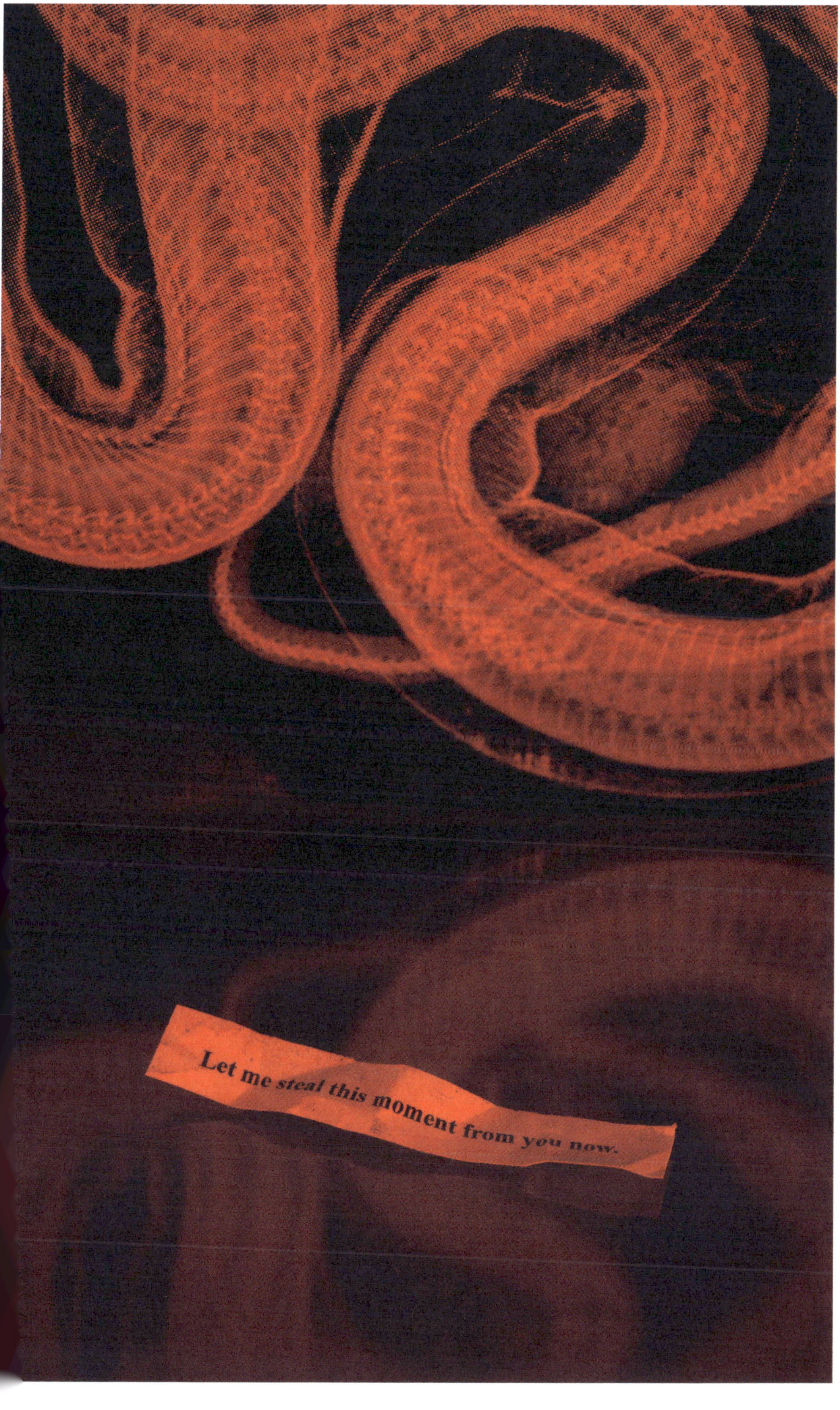
Let me steal this moment from you now.

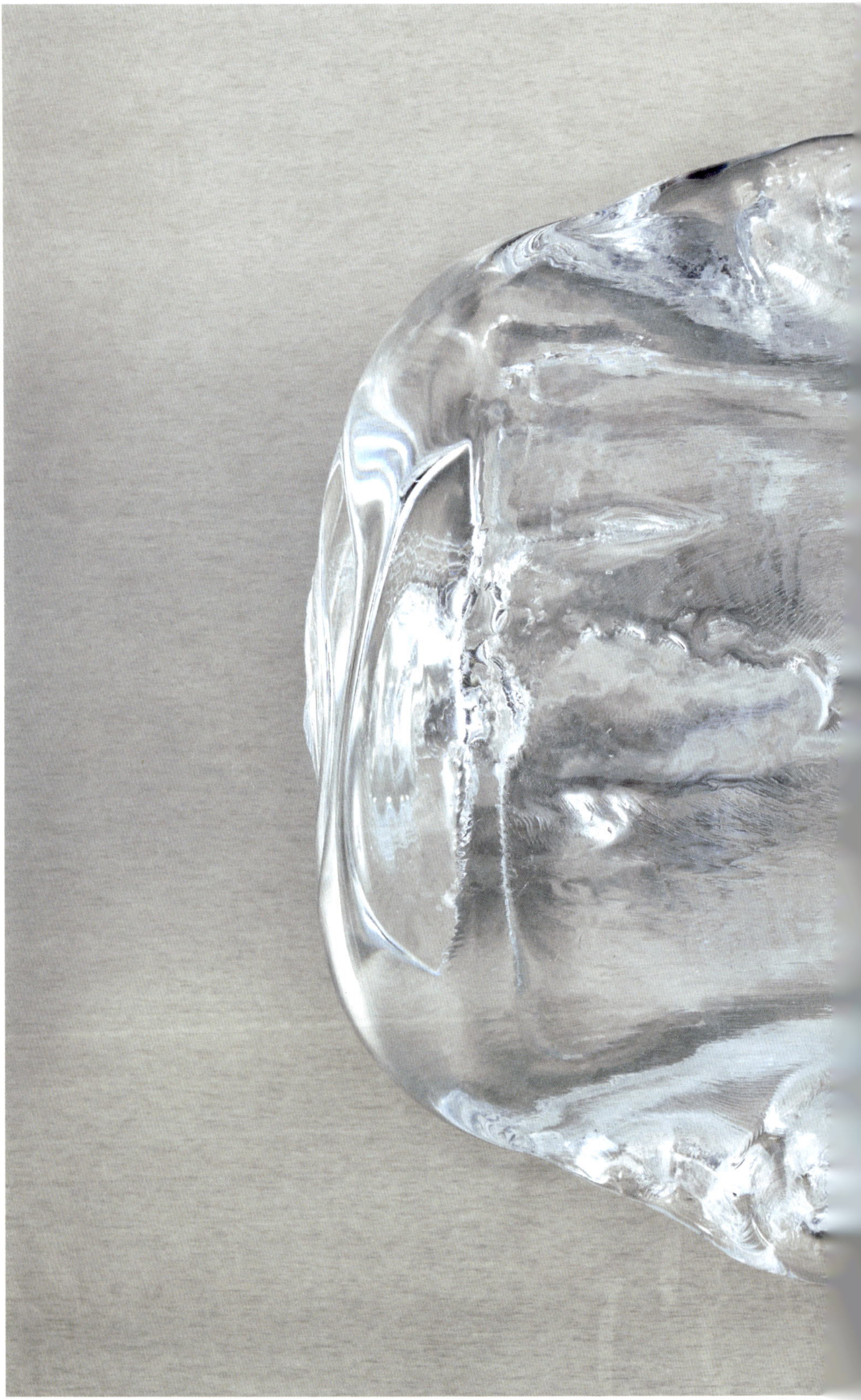

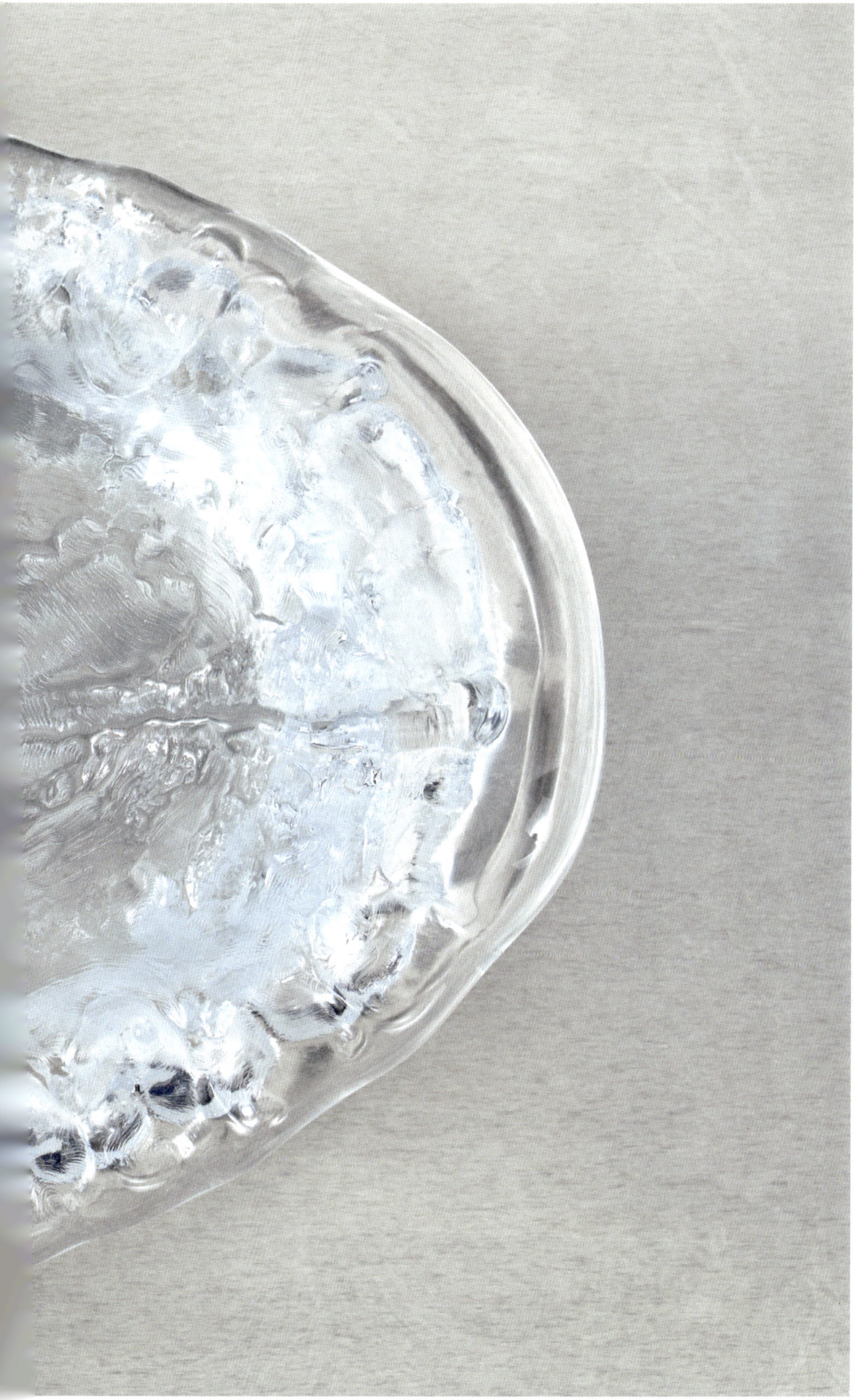

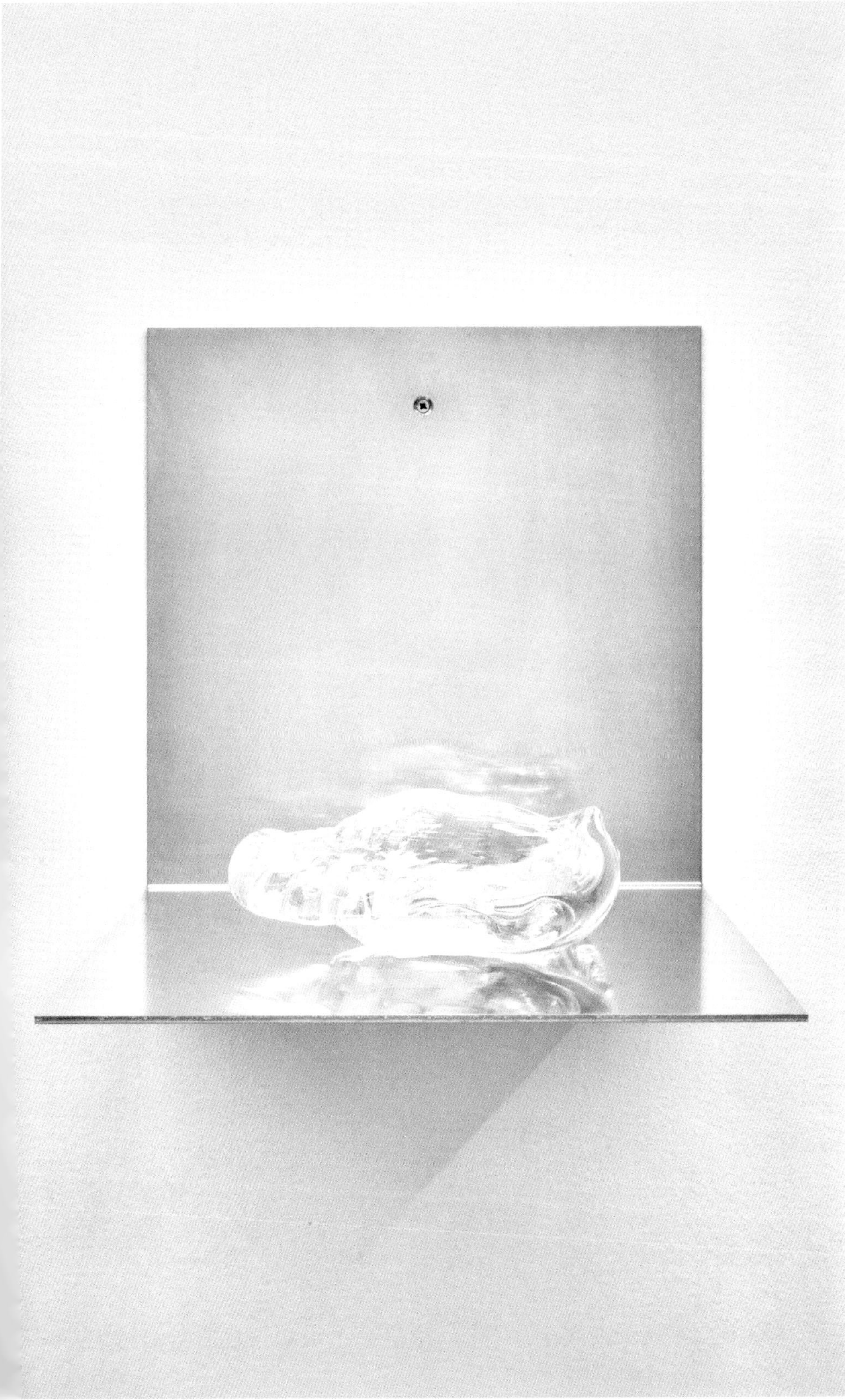

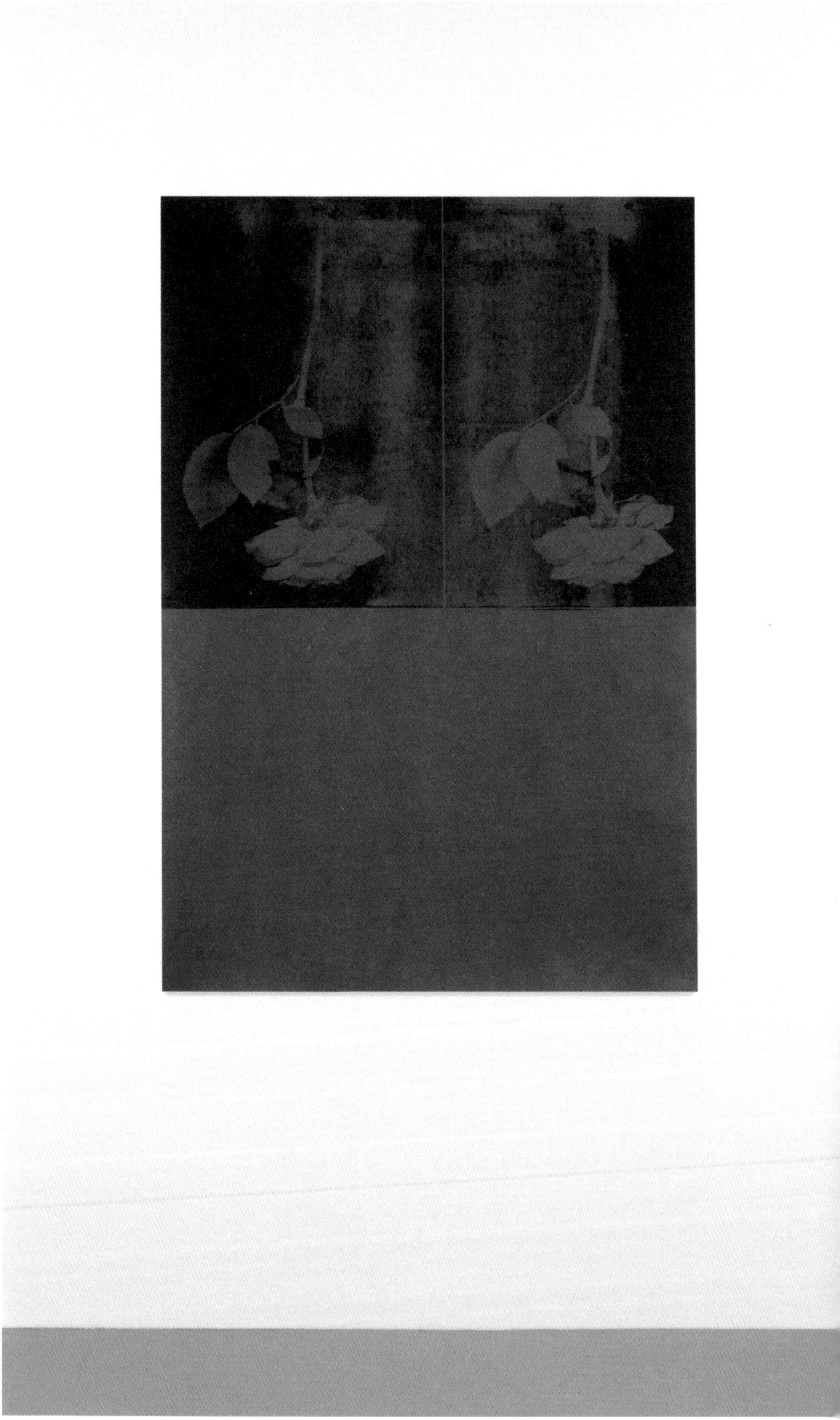

The one time I try to wash my hands
I collapse and feel a city take shape
And probably everyone feels like a bridge
So I wait
The imprinted eye, the neon key
Inherited gifts
Contort to one shape for eternity
And Haunt every surface with a glass touch
So that I never see again
Through the predator lens
Not safe, not yet,
But soon
Alone is My honor To witness
Children holding up branches
Growing a pyramid of spirit
That will flatten
All of This, Everything that built me
So stay very still
You have always believed and you do still
This is the window
I will keep my word

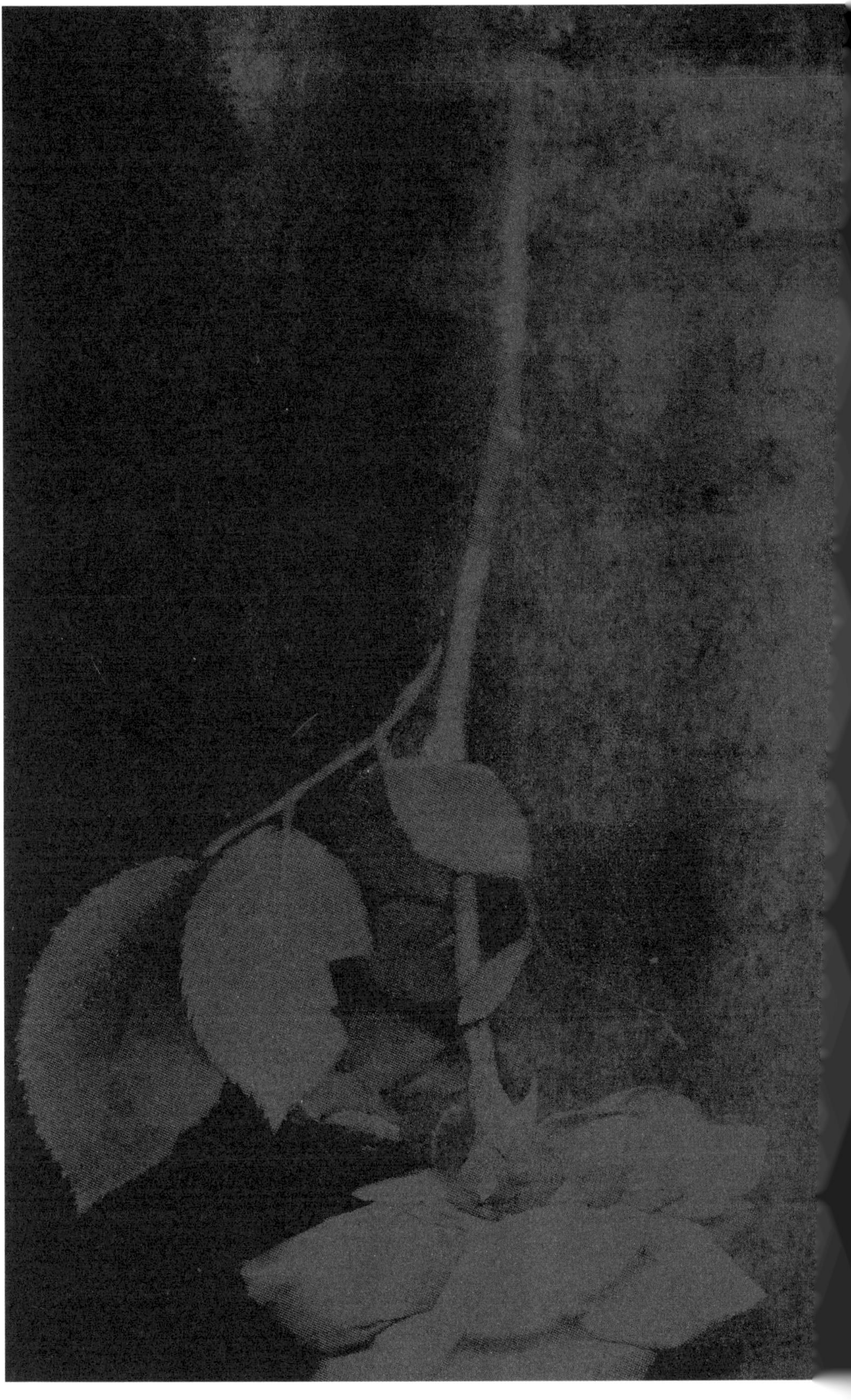

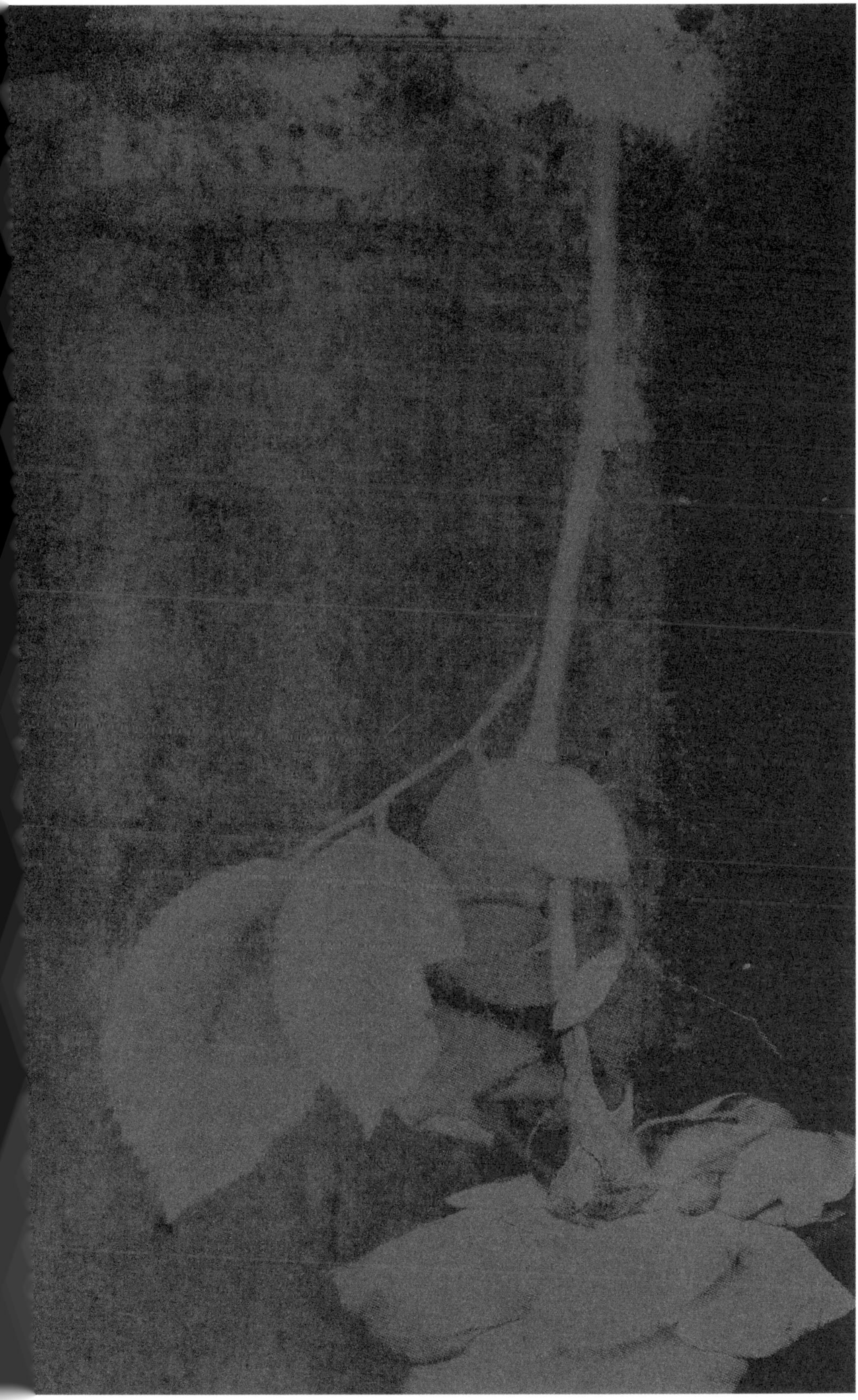

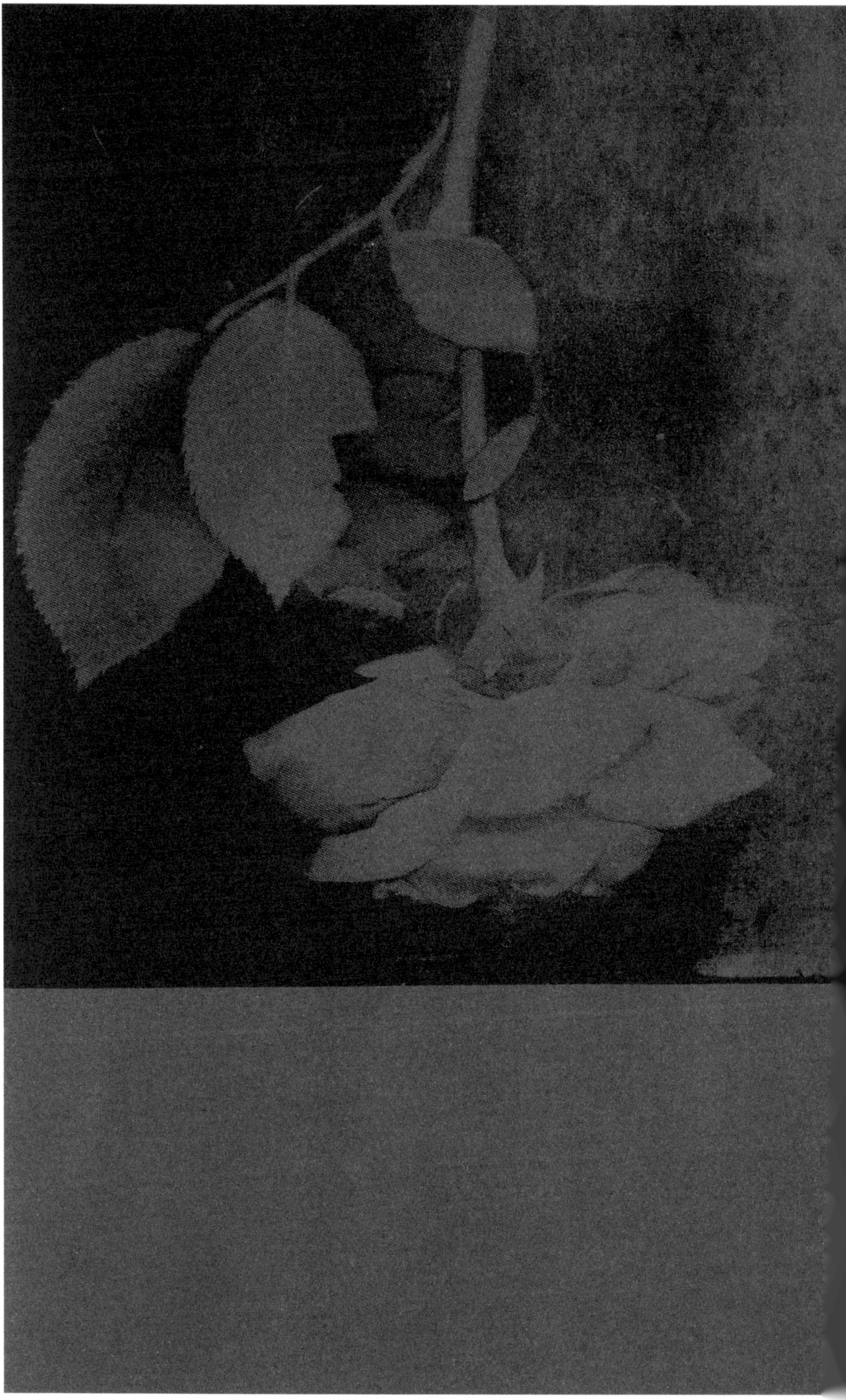

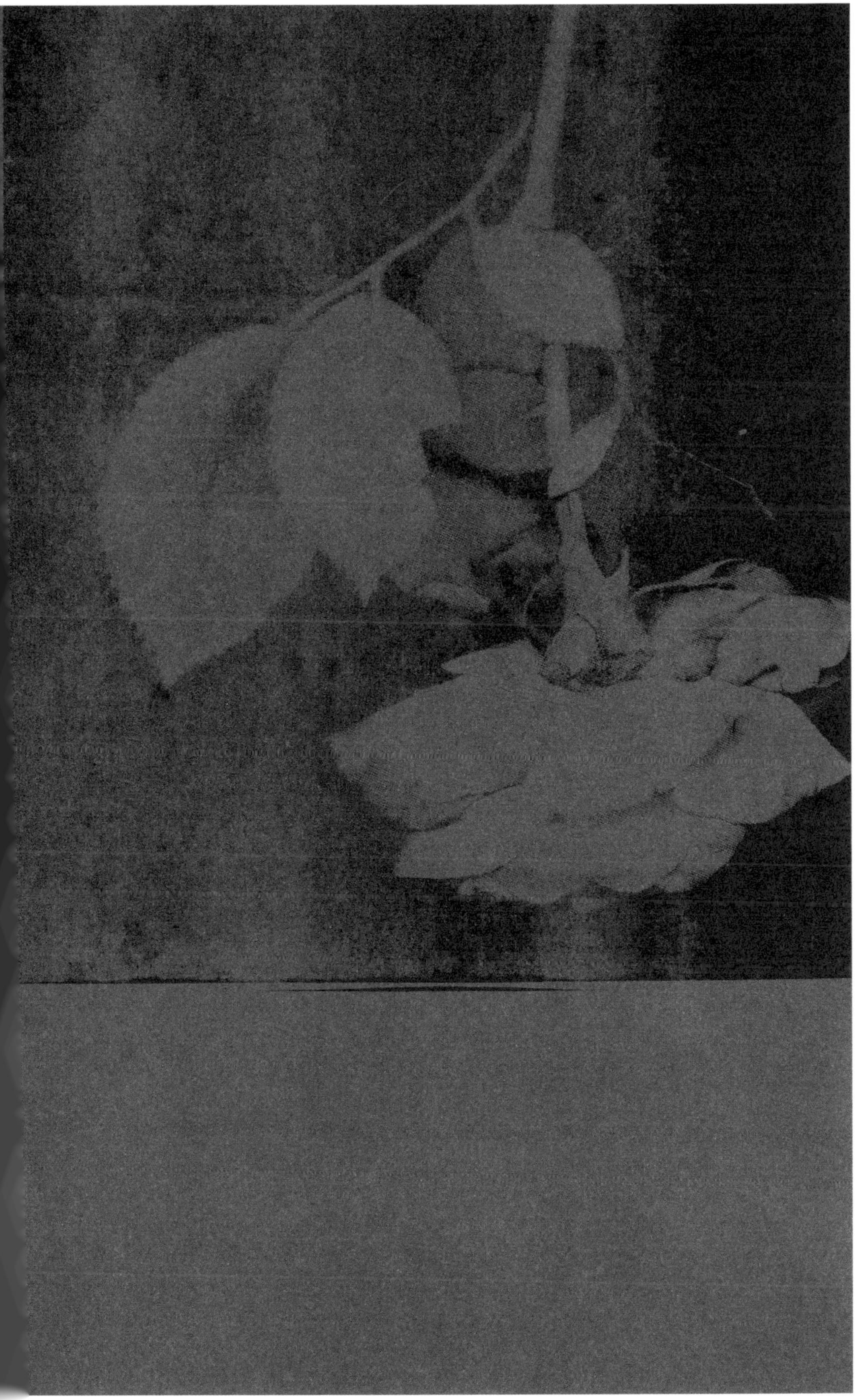

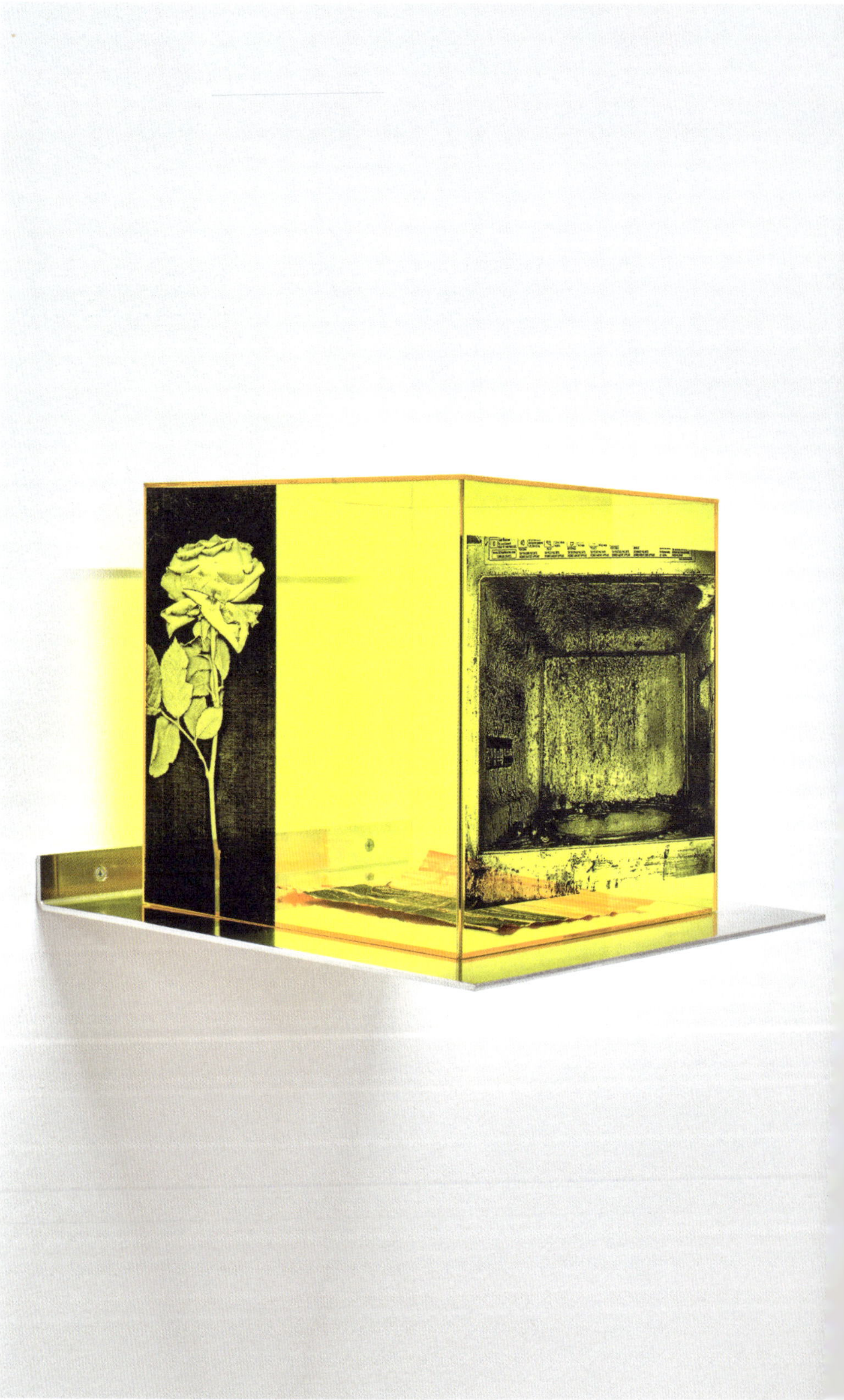

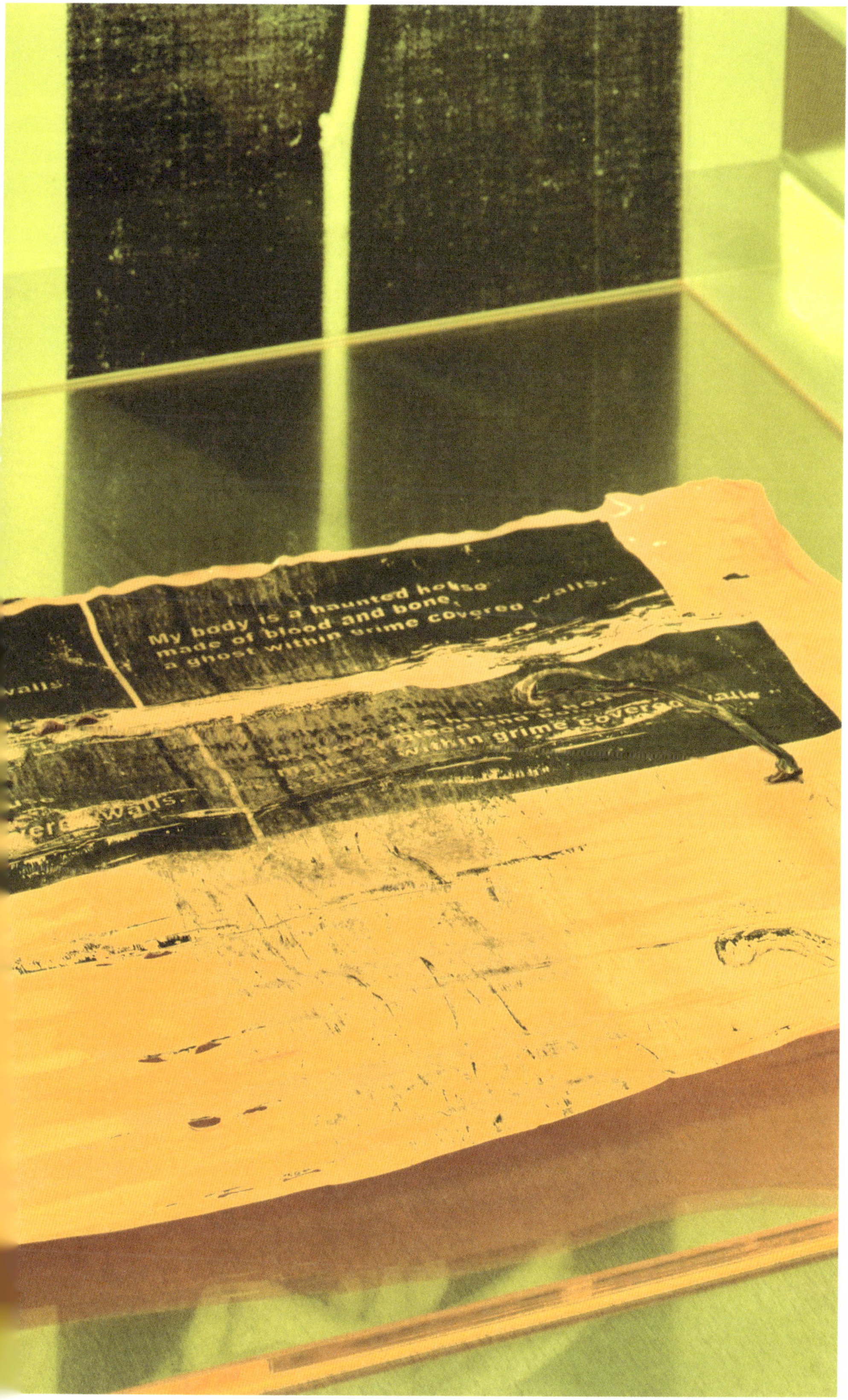
My body is a haunted house
made of blood and bone,
a ghost within grime covered walls.

"The moon has a partial face, trapped to look at us just so,
and another face, always looking away.
[...]
Gaze across the lake and see if you can find me.
Move through fog until we touch."[1]

Something given time to make its absence felt, for its lack to really feel. The conchoidal rifts of obsidian, the gossamer inclusions of phantom quartz: you are a quiet dark shape to yourself, and you see shapes in there. Pause to place your hand over ice. The freeze swirls into itself, clear ice on clear ice is a frenzy of tendrils and cracks, where the whitest whites are just smaller splits, crystal branchlets writing arabesques. Like how hoarfrost patterns occur on the skin—Lichtenberg figures—caused by lightning strikes. "Dust figures," "skin feathering" or "lightning flowers," they call them. In its disarray of fractal breaks, ice rouses legibility as mere false relief. Like darkness, its multiplicity tremors lost and recalcitrant into absorbent depths. Black watercolor floating out from a brush dipped in water. Species of void one can't help but hold onto; a coldness that is lethal at first, slowly warms to the touch.

It's true: "So many things seem to locate themselves in lack."[2] I'm talking about deep depth, about hiddenness. Voids are irrepressible confessions in time to which we are hopelessly tethered, offering temporary rest for discrepant thoughts. Vacancy a space carved out for provisional relief. That anonymity. In extremity, things achieve a different texture and thus different feedback. Darkness, for instance, allows for things to lift precisely for its incommensurability. Night thoughts.

The resignation of philosophical darkness suggests time has reached a full stop, but here it is more like an ellipsis. Lapsed materialities, deformed conductivities, neutered futurities. New materials breed new mysticisms. Scored like glyphic

1
T Fleischmann, *Time Is the Thing a Body Moves Through* (Minneapolis: Coffee House Press, 2019), 97.
2
Ibid., 37.

hearts in bark, somber and slightly doomsday punctuations are timorous testimonies of desired permanence: rainwater's *soft sorrow*. The tremulous promise of rain, it tingles and interferes. Rain, in fact, makes you feel weightless, everything compressed and splintered at once, a sensitizing shelter within which you are a mere effect. You feel mutable. The rain sharpens and depletes you into multiplying, evanescent densities; I guess that's why people feel "liberated."

"A nocturnal robe of obsidian draped over our most precious, most anonymous thoughts."[3] Yes, this psychology is contoured in cloaks, scantily spiritual in the way that gloom's lethargy becomes climatological. In gloom, we linger: "Gloom is the horror of a hovering stasis that is life."[4] Steeping in ovate dreams beneath a dying sky, this mind is an atmosphere that permeates surroundings, seeing in the world languorous behaviors. You hold an ear to the disinterested world, knowing that its opaque force bites back. Less the sun's "mental ejaculation"[5] than its secreted eclipse, the revelation of its giving up. Such lonely immersions are rare nowadays, but for those of us similarly alienated, it's always already there. You trace affection for a world-without-us, the cosmic negativity that remains after us.

"To become overgrown, like a ruin."[6] These remains testify to what once was, things that cannot be lost in a simple way. Ambivalent they skirt the realm of the *reliquiae*, yet are not resigned to its calcified finality. Their anti-vanitas vibe welcomes the solemnity of remnants and the deliberation of debris. Each saturnine vessel suggests a fiction of containment, when really, they open out the intrasubjective. Interiorities made almost radically skinless, x-rayed and see-through.

3
Eugene Thacker, *Infinite Resignation* (London: Repeater Books, 2018), 59.

4
Eugene Thacker, *Cosmic Pessimism* (Minneapolis: Univocal Publishing, 2015), 21.

5
Georges Bataille, *Visions of Excess* (Minneapolis: University of Minnesota Press, 1970; 1985), 57.

6
Thacker, *Cosmic Pessimism*, 54.

Echinate enigmas, their exposed teeth and blind implacable eye snatching contact. This interior mind, absent of a body, is potent enough to function as a descriptor of what is not there—an infinite absence where no language is adequate and where philosophic thought collapses. At last: we are all openly encrypted to each other, to ourselves. Exquisite, sundered hopelessness. The bared outline of a single subject loosens into the onyx murk of a glowering emptiness. This open, deep-sleep state of self-world relation is an invitation to intimacy that sustains private symbolisms. If it is a way of seeing the world in the same frame as an individual body, or a thought, it is a pessimistic diffusion of psyche and world: "A solipsism that is also the ultimate form of empathy with the unhuman. The one fantasy pessimism allows itself—the sadness of the cosmos."[7]

Unplaceable, time is abeyant here, with forms collecting about an orphaned sense of "after" unlocatable in its loss like melancholy. In melancholia, the loss cannot be situated; it has been obscured and recovery deferred seemingly into infinity. Coiling, the severed melancholic gaze turns inward because the silhouette one wants to fill is simply unknown, its object of loss only half-alive. For Walter Benjamin, melancholy is not discontinuous with mourning, less a pathological condition than an activated attitude that symbolically brings the loss inside, to rest. This work, "from the realm of mourning to that of meaning," as Ilit Ferber writes, expresses "a deepening of the loss, an extended deadening of the object from which a fullness surfaces".[8] The retention and intensification of loss rather than its expulsion and overcoming. With their future extracted, one might figure these works as collections of detachments that, following Ferber's analysis of Benjamin's melancholic engagement, undertake *expression* to make the object of loss *present*. "Consequently," Ferber continues, "detachment here means presentation and not concealment or

7 Thacker, *Infinite Resignation*, 66.

8 Ilit Ferber, "Melancholy Philosophy: Freud and Benjamin," *EREA* 4.1 (Spring 2006), 66–74.

suppression."[9] In this state of full expressivity, the object is drained of life… rested, deadened, buried, frozen. Utterly delivered to a point of standstill, these are the small deaths we collect.

In the aftermath that are these stilled forms, tentatively held at a remove, is this processual melancholy of bringing disunities to rest, which might be ascribed to Ferber's "deepening death." These disidentifications and disharmonies are unresolved, commemoratively laid out like prefigured wounds. In this self-world, work is the observance of potentiality at the point of its evacuation of meaning. At the futile vector of asking: *What's left?* Empty dimensions cleave deep impressions.

These reflections are surely a pursual of intimacy, to sense in one's lack what has been lost and to enfold within writing so many unconsummated and lingering thoughts, images, intimacies. Seeking reverberations of oneself within the other is an irreducible undertaking that goes both ways—I cull the thought from Moyra Davey: "I am reliant on the words of others, and I glom on to the dead."[10] Stalagmite attachments in a system of echoes, the "so many things" of lack. In these instants, we plumb for oneself as much as someone else. The continued failure to internalize the other leads once more to the orientations of "want" and "desire" to which one might turn toward even at the risk of further loss—a process that paradoxically affirms a sense of aliveness. These are the strange demands of intimacy's distances—that it might require further takings-in, takings-on. The want for that impossible "without," for unhuman thought and remote continuity, where the moon looks away—it is in this atmospheric site of inner life where I am met, making contact through the fog.

9
Ibid.
10
Moyra Davey, *Index Cards* (London: Fitzcarraldo Editions, 2020), 188.

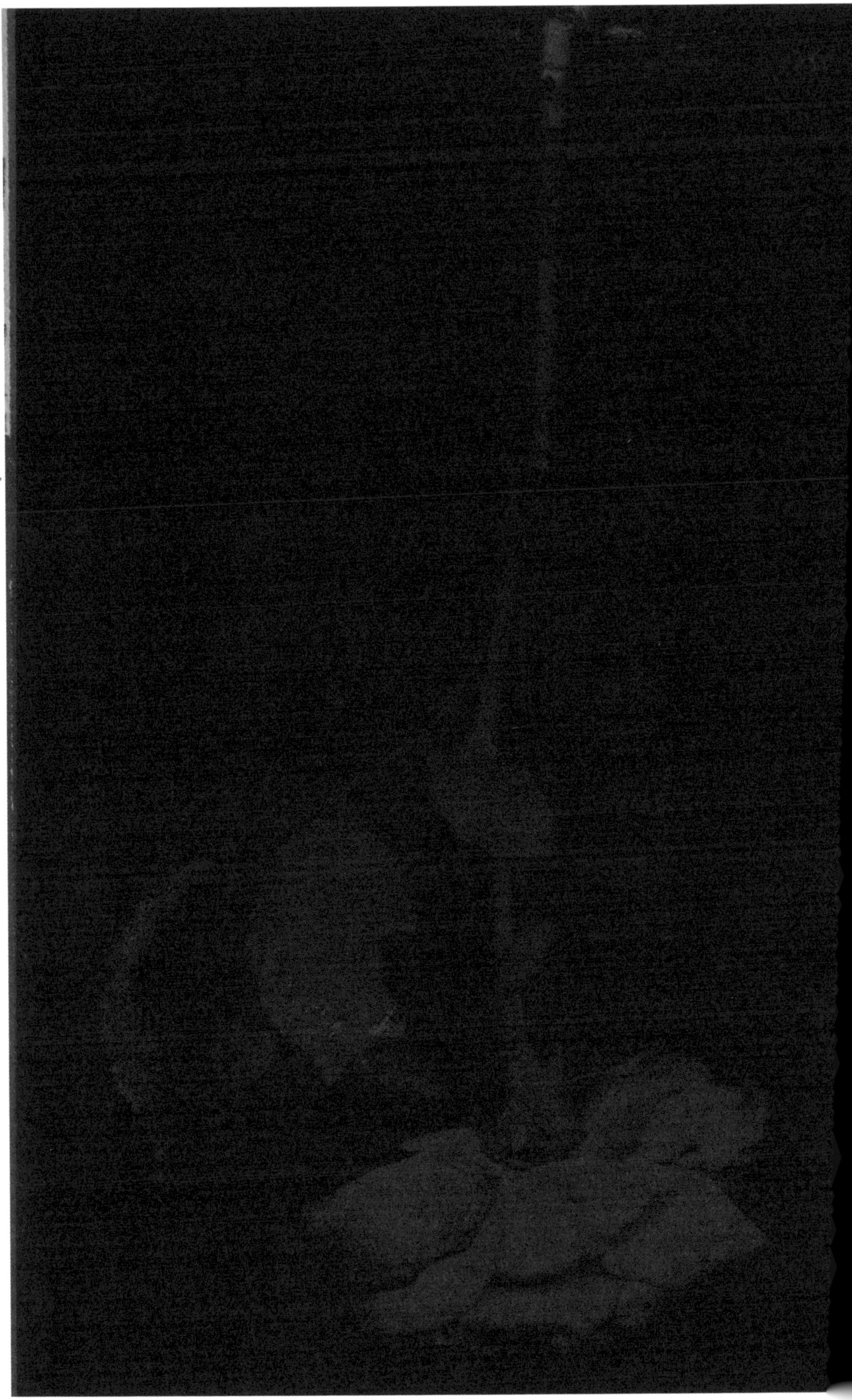

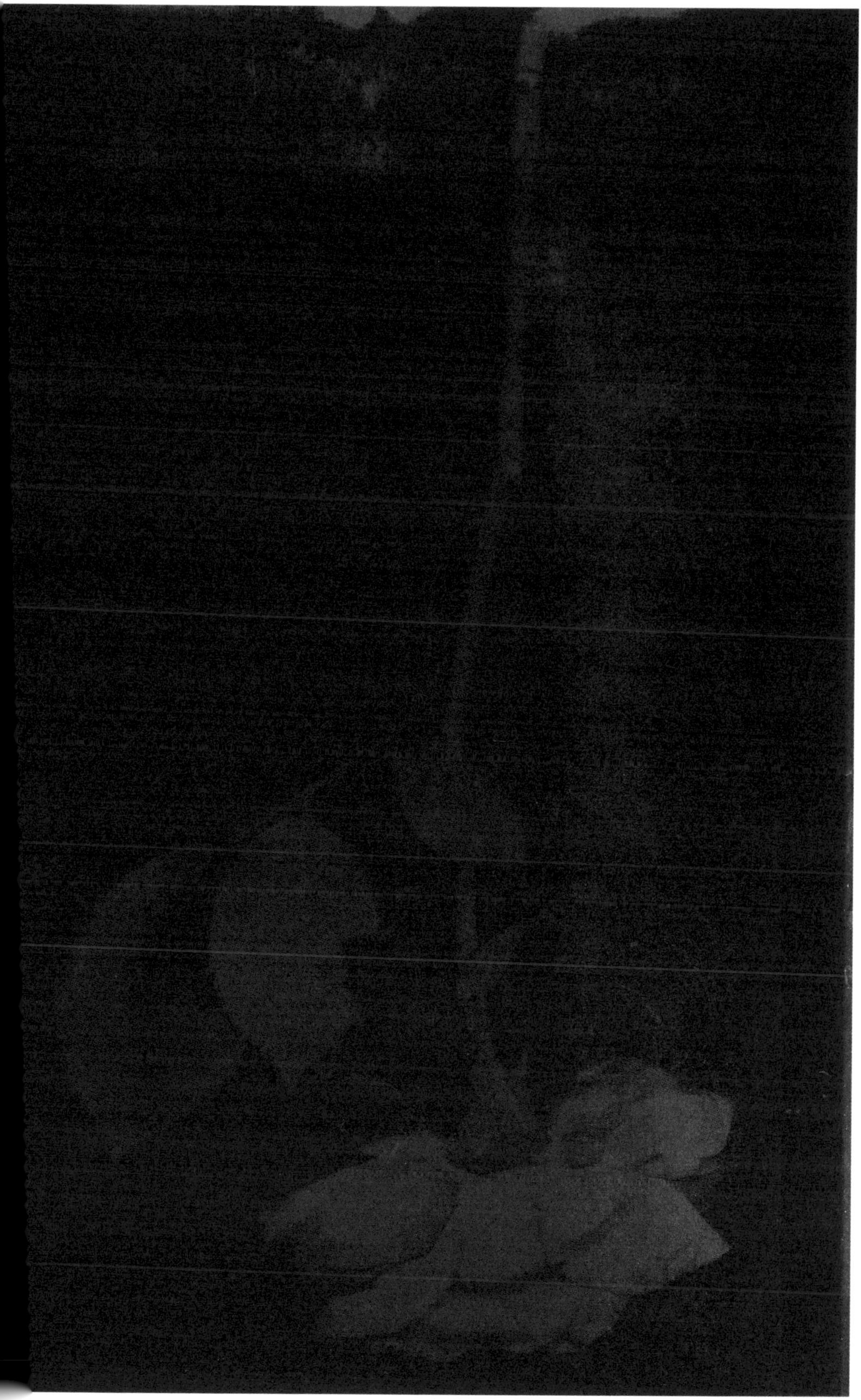

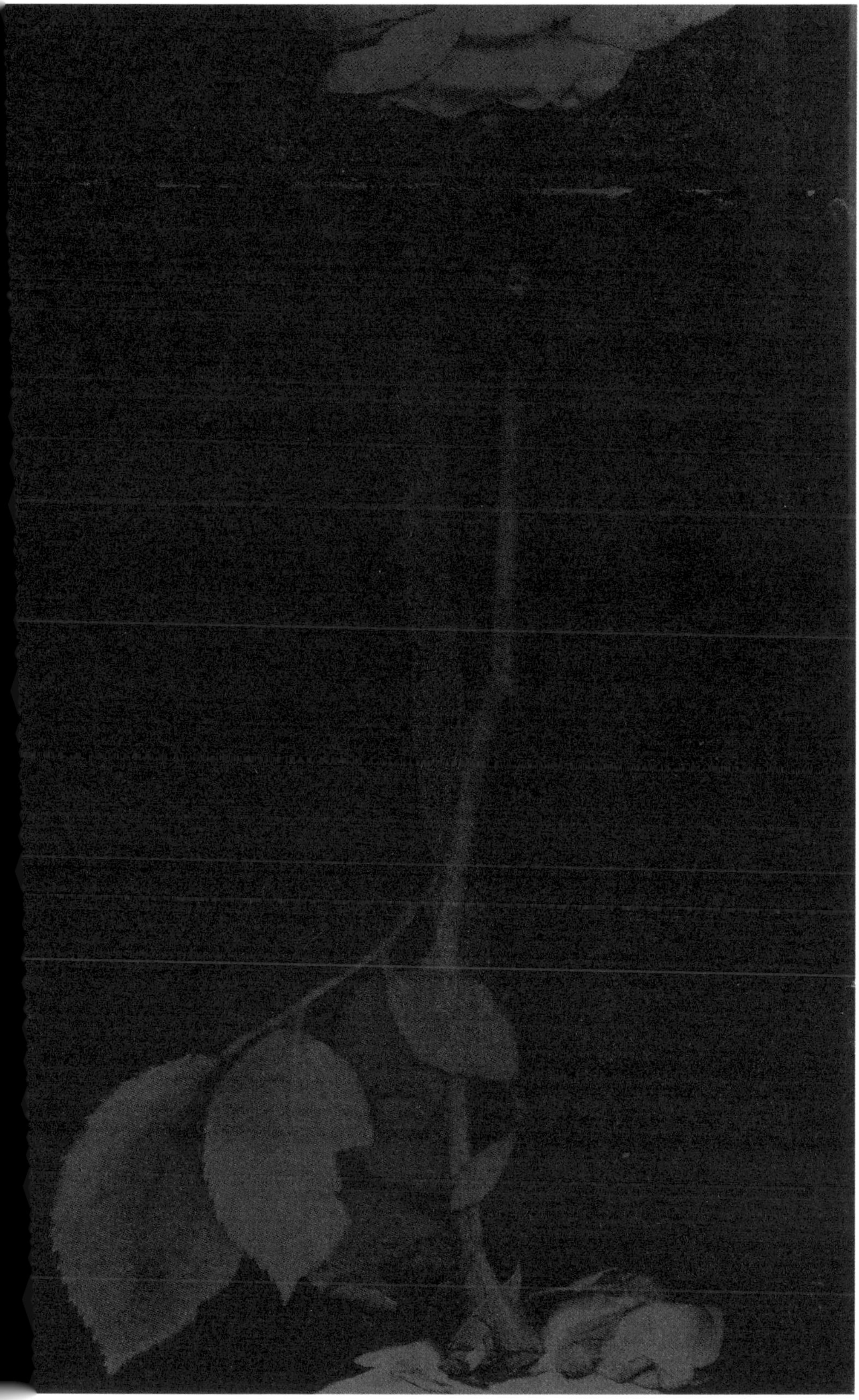

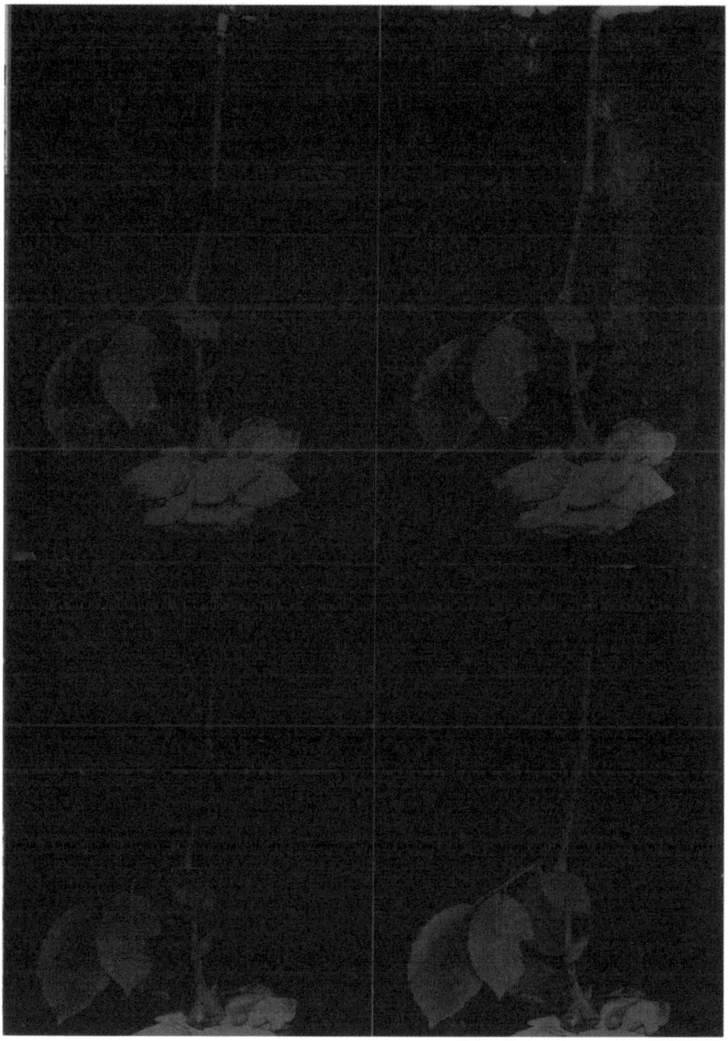

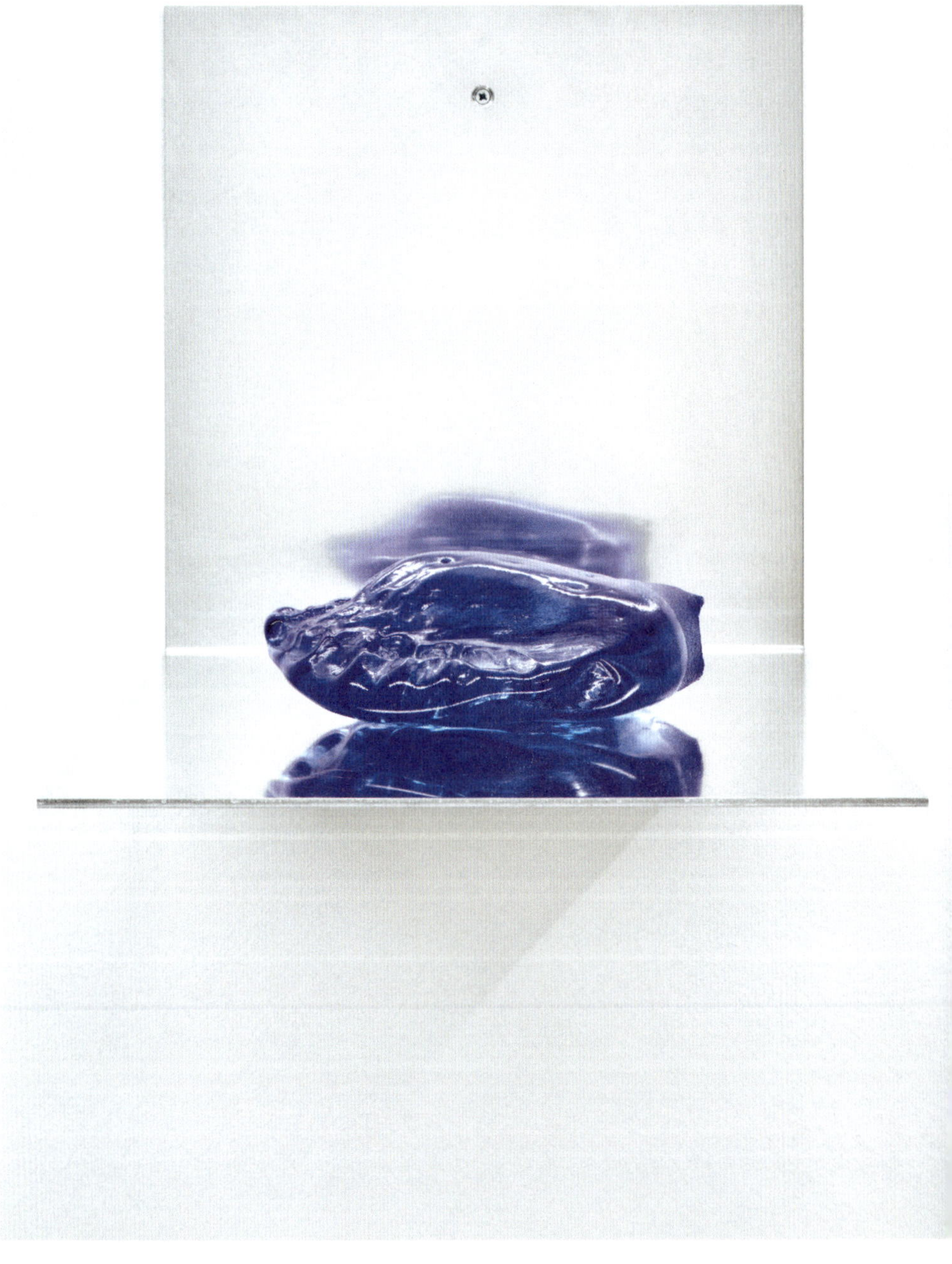

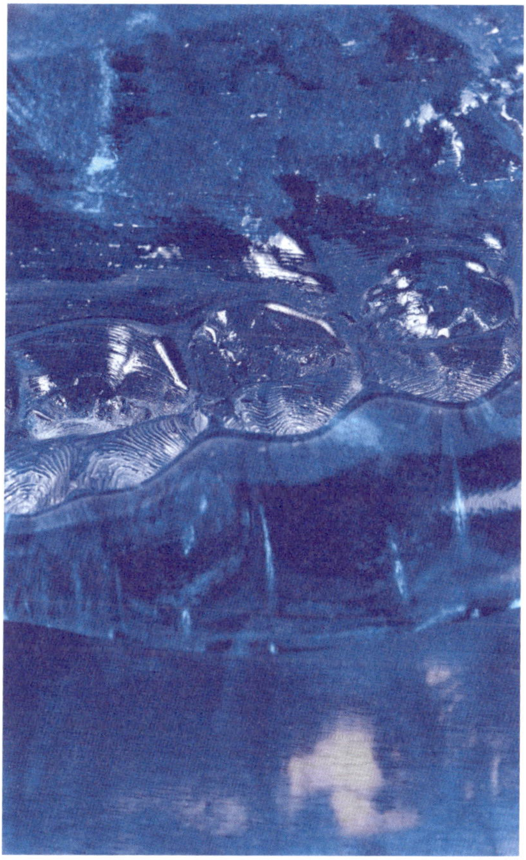

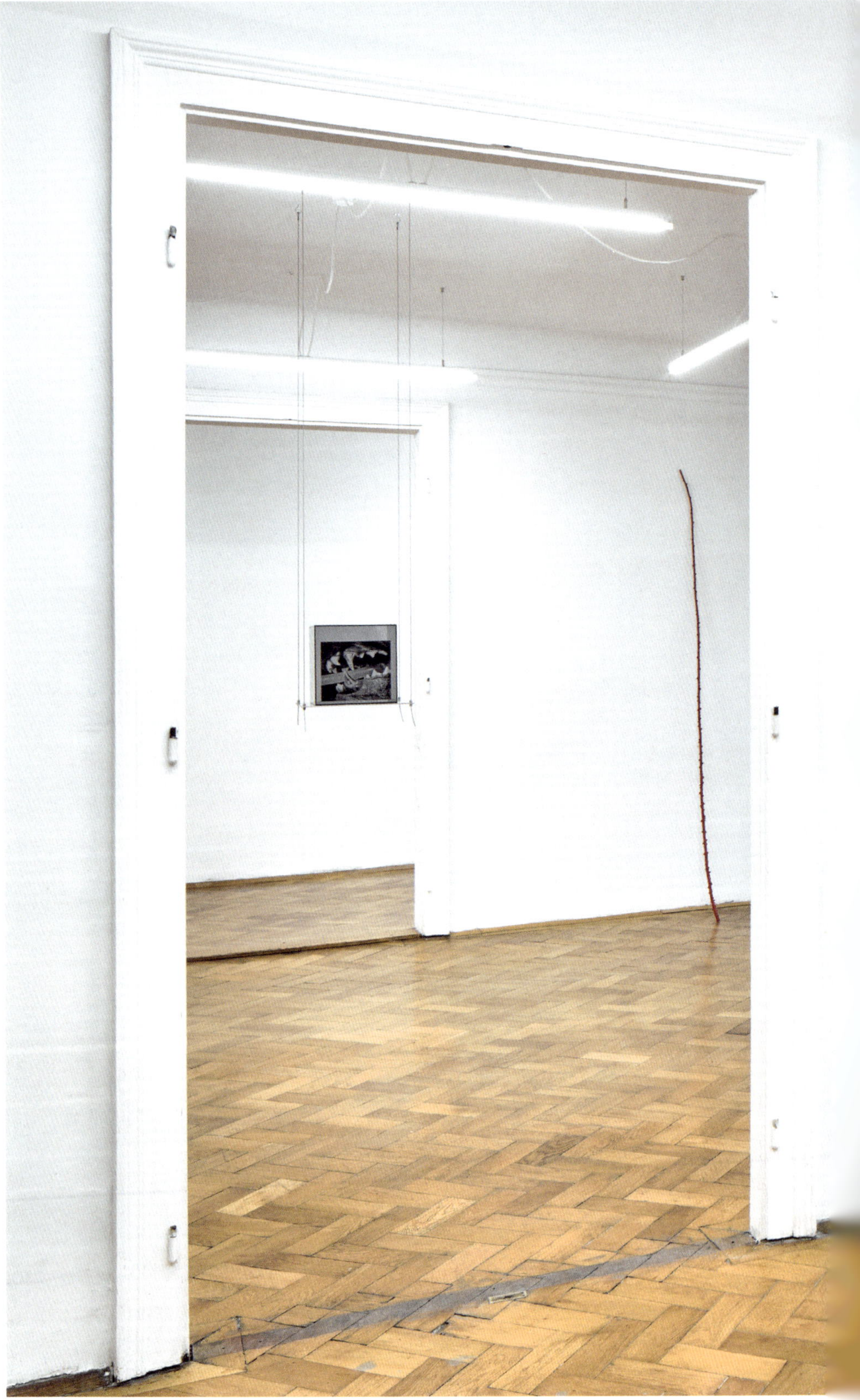

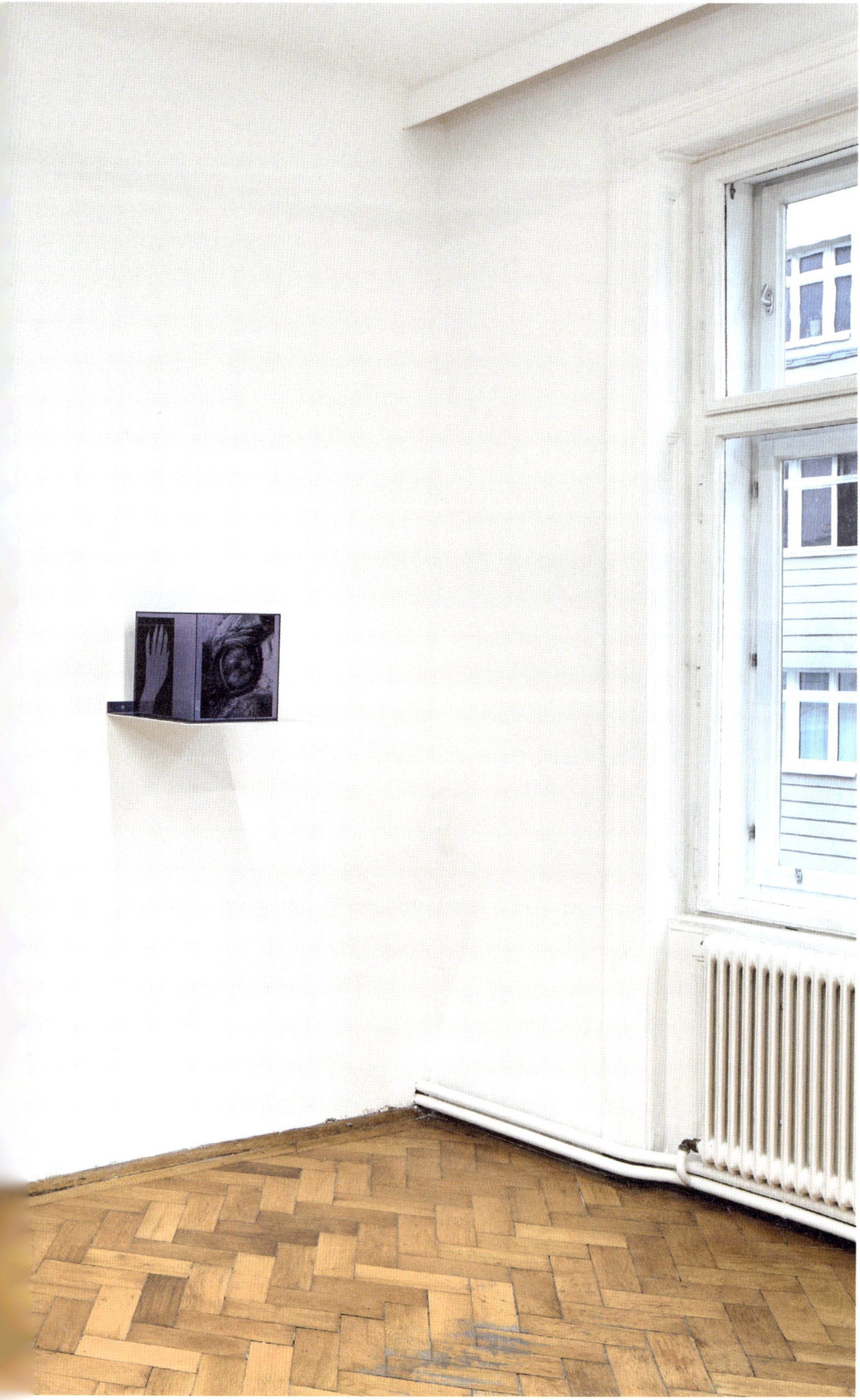

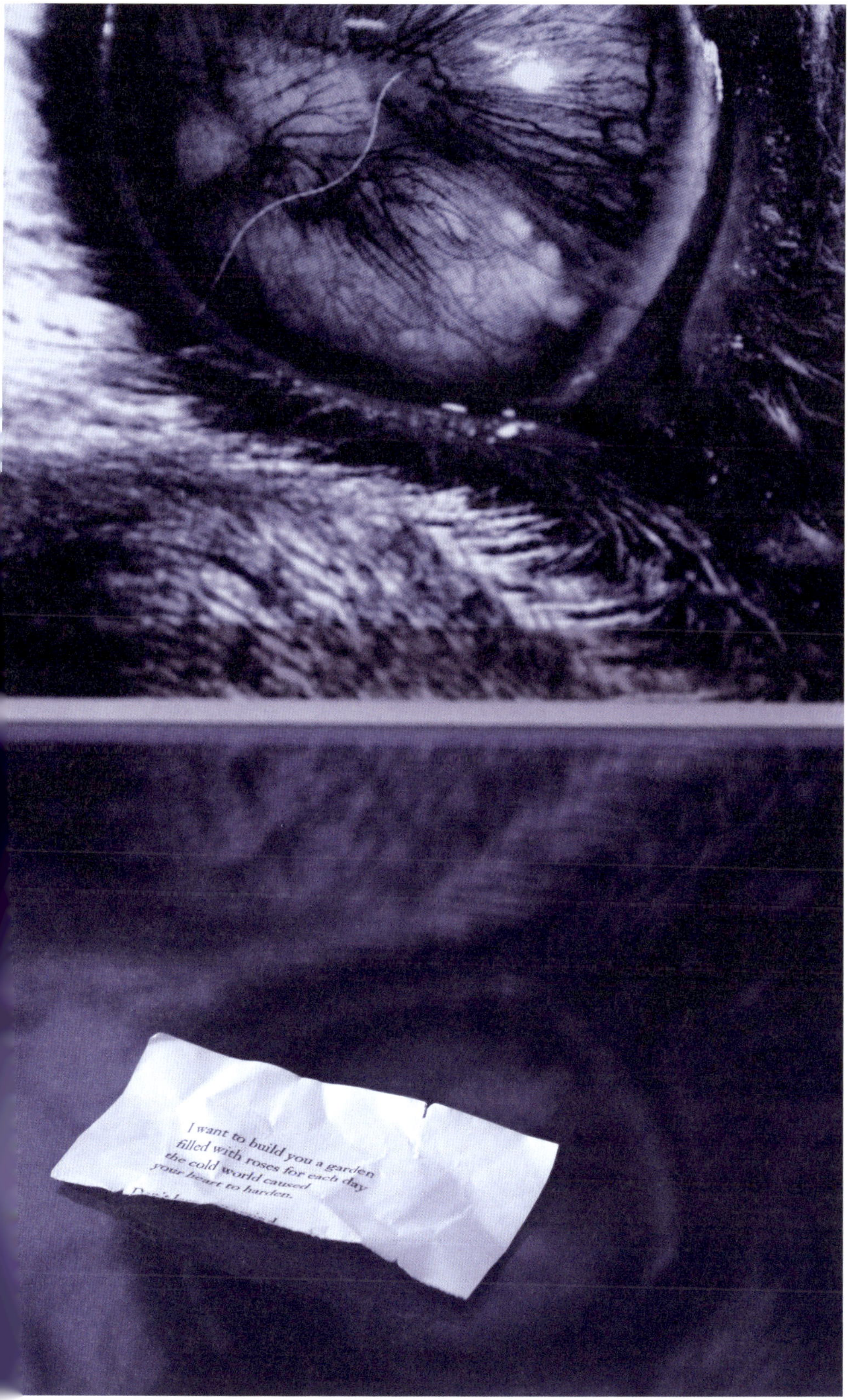
I want to build you a garden
filled with roses for each day
the cold world caused
your heart to harden.

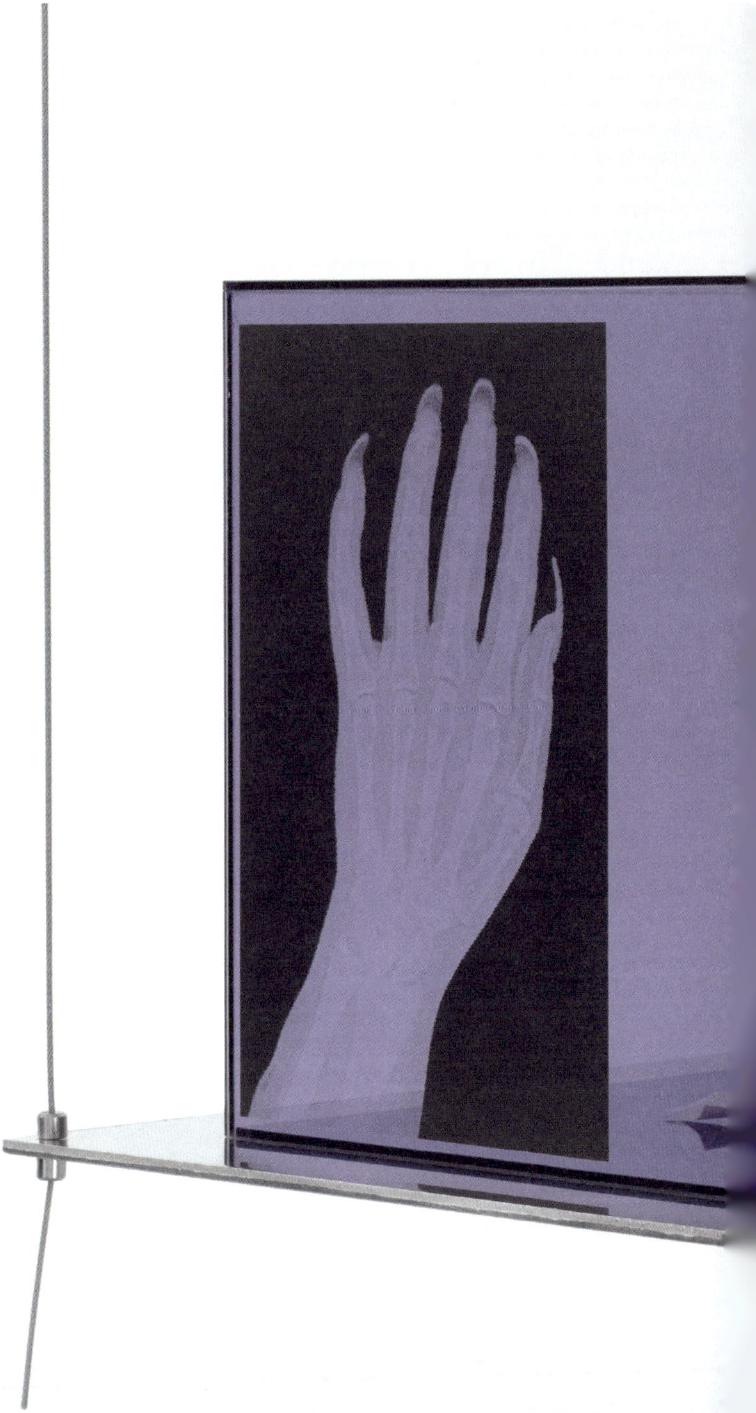

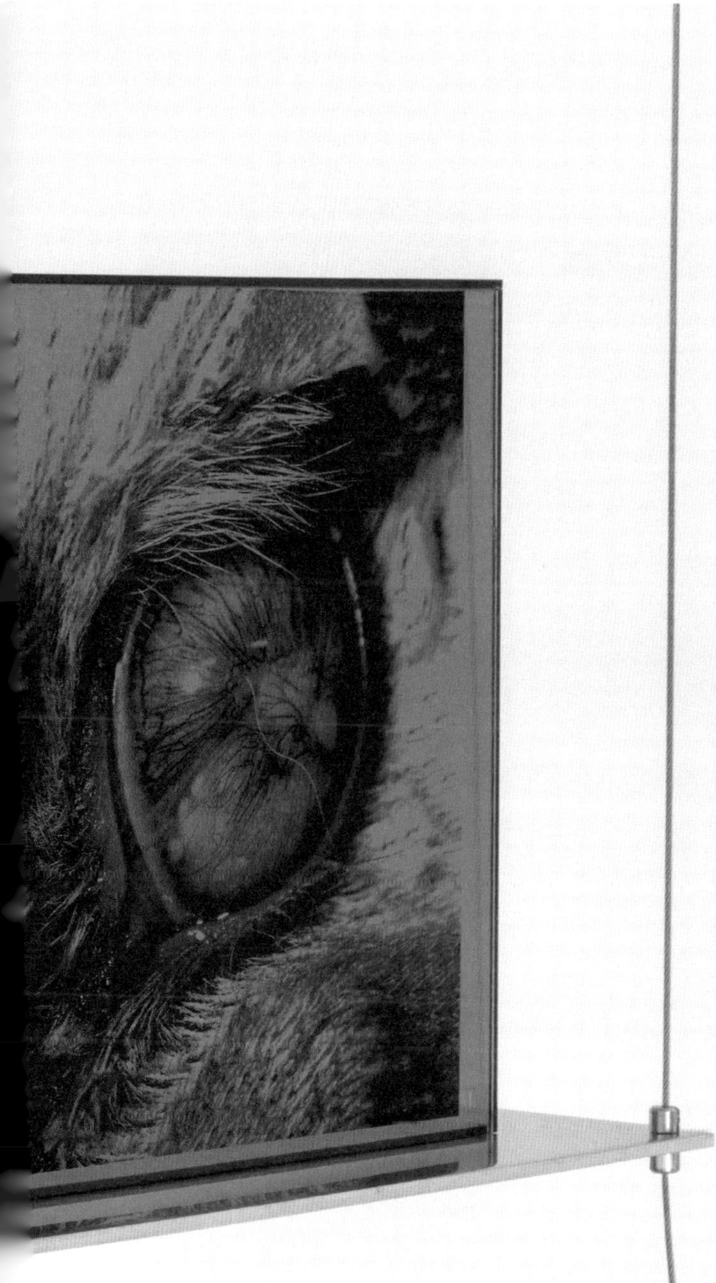

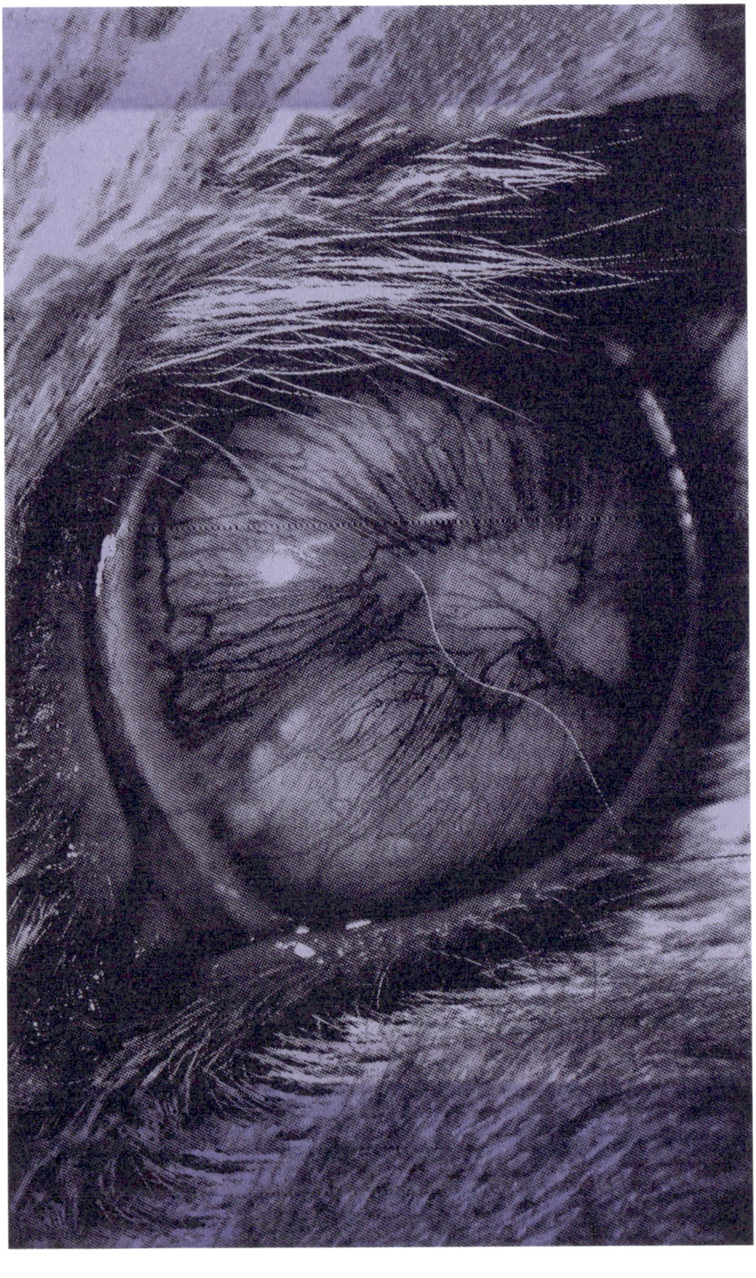

The starting point for the publication *Nervous Dust* is Martin Maeller's solo exhibition of the same title, held at Kunstverein Göttingen in 2022. This publication offers the first comprehensive overview of Martin's artistic work and his intensive and persistent examination of experiences of loss, alienation, and the search for belonging. Contributions from writers and artists provide deeper insights into themes visible in Martin's work. The perspectives presented here bring together contexts and ideas in a multifaceted way and unfold in a critical manner.

Martin's work combines personal experiences, text, and elements of pop and subculture to observe subjective and collective states of psychological and physical tension. Spanning a diverse array of media, including printmaking, sculpture, and installations, his practice constructs inner worlds between melancholy and loss, affection and care. His visual and conceptual language presents fleeting moments that form spaces of resonance for individual consciousness.

Martin alienates and fragments overlooked and unconventional objects, transforming and giving them new meaning. His works are frequently charged with art- and cultural-historical references and appear slick and reduced, yet also intimate and intuitive. Through his use of industrial and organic materials, as well as personal and anonymous objects, Martin's work creates seemingly eerie atmospheres where a sense of familiarity is rarely found.

He poetically questions the way in which identity is constructed and emphasizes the sensitivity and vulnerability inherent in it. He blurs notions of social conventions, at times pointing to those who feel cut off from the world due to their own identity. His work touches on queer culture, power dynamics, and the intricate interplay between humanity and the natural world. It opens up a spiritual realm that remains elusive in the uncanny, and brings forth unusual forms of remembrance and commemoration that contrast with the physical world. The work interrogates and reflects on what is given value or is deemed worthy of being memorialized.

Martin repeatedly formulates narratives that deliberately collapse into contradictions. By incorporating individual codes and loose definitions, he draws attention to ambivalent moments and thus creates places of power. His work focuses on inner, undiscovered worlds that, as a result of their exclusion, lie outside of common ways of seeing. With his artistic work, he therefore deciphers and maps the dark terrain of the unconscious and focuses on reclaiming personal agency.

This publication is the result of an intensive, but above all committed and close, collaboration. Martin and I would like to thank everyone involved, especially Samuel Bänziger, who found the right form for this publication. Thanks to Bunny Rogers for the first release of her poem Seafoam from 2022 and P. Staff's poetic contribution, which was completed especially for this publication. Thanks also to Alex Bennett for the contribution, which illuminates the emotional darkness and encourages to shine a light on its veiled beauty. Philipp Hindahl's carefully chosen words, which do not disappoint the melancholic, and Cathrin Mayer for the precise formulations and thoughts on Martin's work. We would like to thank everyone for the trust they placed in this project.

Appendix

German Translations
List of Works
Colophon

Dunkle Ecken
Philipp Hindahl

Bedenkt man, dass manche den – pathologischen – Zustand der Melancholie als *asymbolique* (asymbolisch) bezeichnen, ist erstaunlich, wie viel darüber geschrieben wird. Dabei wäre es ziemlich schwer, nur über die Melancholie zu schreiben; sie ist kein Thema an sich. Für Betroffene durchdringt sie alles. Sie verändert die Wahrnehmung der Welt grundsätzlich. Was über Melancholie geschrieben wird, ist immer auch aus der Melancholie heraus geschrieben, als wäre die Sprache selbst vergiftet, und als würde der Zustand Zeichen, Wörter und Sätze betreffen.

Alles wurde schon einmal von jemandem empfunden. Der Autor Robert Burton listet in *Die Anatomie der Melancholie* (1988; orig. 1621) die möglichen Ursachen der Melancholie auf. Manche sind übernatürlich, wie Hexen und Magier; andere sind natürlichen Ursprungs, wie Sternkonstellationen, das Lebensalter oder von den Eltern vererbte Charakterzüge. Einige sind selbstverschuldet, wie schlechte Ernährung oder Trunksucht. Und dann nennt Burton Selbstliebe, Stolz und Angeberei. Die eitle Einbildung auf die eigenen guten Eigenschaften sei eine aktive Ursache der Melancholie. Wir bewundern, schmeicheln und applaudieren uns wie Narziss, schreibt Burton: „Was ist eine Stadt für ein Königreich, ein Königreich für Europa, Europa für die Welt und was ist die Welt selbst, die ein Ende hat sobald man sie mit dem kleinsten sichtbaren Stern am Firmament vergleicht, der achtzehnmal größer ist als sie?“[1] Wer melancholisch ist, bekommt ein Gefühl für die Ewigkeit – oder auch nicht. Spätestens seit dem Mittelalter sind Melancholiker kosmologisch an den Saturn gebunden, weil sie im Schatten dieses Zeichens zur Welt kamen. Saturn entsendet Partikel, die die ganze Welt ihrem Bann unterwerfen, wie schwarze Galle, die den Körper durchdringt. Man kann sich Saturn als den nächtlichen Statthalter der Sonne vorstellen, einen ängstlichen, bitteren und einsamen Gott ohne eigenen Thron.

Die Melancholie steht einer Zeit entgegen, die das Metaphysische zum Verschwinden bringen will und das Unmögliche versucht: das eigene Denken von dunklen Ecken zu befreien und ein gnadenloses Regime des Wohlbefindens einzuführen, während sie alle verborgenen Winkel bereinigt. Melancholie ist ein tiefes Heimweh nach den zwielichtigen Flecken, und diese Sehnsucht schmerzt, weil sie für immer unerfüllt bleibt. Melancholie ist das verborgene Gesicht des Narziss, die andere Seite seiner Selbstliebe. Das früh verwundete Selbst drückt sich in Schwermut aus. Aber darüber hinaus hat die Melancholie mit Liebe zu tun – Liebe zu einem verlorenen Objekt; sie ist die Trauer um das Mutterobjekt, so nennt es die Psychoanalyse. Man liebt und man hasst, denn zu lieben ist die Angst, das Andere zu verlieren.

Zu den wahrscheinlich schönsten Arbeiten, die die Melancholie hervorgebracht hat, zählt das Inventar der Tränen des Komponisten John Dowland aus dem Jahr 1604 mit dem schlichten Titel *Lachrimae*. Die Musik läuft Gefahr, lächerlich zu wirken, wäre da nicht die Selbstreflexion in den Titeln der langsamen Stücke: Er nennt sie, vielleicht nicht ganz ohne Humor, *Alte Tränen*, *Neue Tränen*, *Traurige Tränen*. Anders als Orpheus, dessen Musik Gottheiten, Steine und die gesamte Natur zum Weinen brachte, entlockt Dowland Plutos Wange keine eisernen Tränen. Warum zieht es die Menschen zur Trauer? Möglicherweise ist sie das Mittel gegen die Einsamkeit, weil sie die eigenen Gefühle widerspiegelt. Vielleicht reinigt sie und hat eine kathartische Wirkung.

In Dowlands Liedersammlung kommt aber noch etwas Modernes zum Vorschein. Wie ein Pop-Album bündelt sie traurige Stücke, und wie ein Echo durch die Jahrhunderte hallen sie bis heute nach. Das letzte Stück Dowlands heißt *Semper Dowland, semper dolens* – ewig Dowland, ewig im Schmerz, zugleich ein Bekenntnis zum Selbstmitleid, dieser besonderen Form des Narzissmus, und eine Klage über verlorene Liebe.

Ich liebe, aber ich hasse mehr noch, und um das Andere nicht zu verlieren, mache ich es mir zu eigen. Aber weil ich es hasse, ist das Andere in mir mein schlechteres Ich. Was bleibt draußen? Das Andere. Es sei denn, man betrachtet die Melancholie, so sehr sie auch mit Selbstliebe zu tun haben mag, als eine Form von Kannibalismus.

1
Hier dt. von der Übersetzerin.

untitled (...)
Vincent Schier

untitled (...)

Drei Dornenranken. Vereinzelt. Unterschiedlich farbig. Die Form ist in ihrer Klarheit verstörend natürlich und unnatürlich irritierend und von einer seltsamen Anziehungskraft. Rot. Chrom. Die Beschichtungen dieser Dornenranken sind genauso beiläufig wie auffällig. Bronze ... genau wie die Legierung, aus der sie gegossen sind. Das Material ist ebenso archaisch wie edel. Beklebt mit einzelnen Stickern zeigen sie einen bewussten menschlichen Eingriff und entziehen sich dennoch einer direkten Einordnung. Was ist es, das diese Dornen trotz ihrer widersprüchlichen Form so vertraut erscheinen lässt?

Dornen sind Teil eines natürlichen Abwehrmechanismus. Gewächse, wie auch der Rosenbusch, tragen Dornen, um Bedrohungen abzuwehren und in ihrer Umgebung bestehen zu können. Wer diese Wehrhaftigkeit überwinden kann, ist oftmals nicht bedrohlich, sondern hat Anteil an einem natürlichen Kreislauf, der das Überleben sichert. Ansonsten gilt es, sich von den abweisenden Dornen fernzuhalten. Dornenranken sind demnach zunächst Abschreckung, sie verursachen eine versinnbildlichte Gefahr, sie warnen vor sich selbst...

(soft sorrow)

Einsam und gleichzeitig ikonisch lehnt die Dornenranke an der Wand. Von übermenschlicher Größe wirkt sie genauso zerbrechlich wie bedrohlich und durchbricht, wie sie verlassen dort steht, Sehgewohnheiten. Als Abguss aus Bronze wirkt die Dornenranke verstörend, unnatürlich, von der Welt abgekapselt, vielleicht sogar fremd. Auf ihr klebt ein Sticker – *soft sorrow* [sanfte Trauer] –, er wirkt ähnlich anklagend wie die Dornenranke selbst. Welche Trauer wird hier beklagt? Und ist es nicht die sanfte Trauer, der wir uns melancholisch hingeben können, die gleichzeitig immer da und dennoch nicht gänzlich greifbar ist?

n der christlichen Ikonografie als Leidenswerkzeug festgeschrieen, ist die Dornenranke zumindest in jenen Gesellschaften, die om christlichen Glauben geprägt sind, aufgeladen mit Bedeuung: Sünde, Leid oder (Selbst-)Geißelung. Es sind biblische chreckensbilder, die sich in der Form der Dornenranke vereinen. ber vor allem ist sie, gebunden als Krone, mit dem Ertragen von eid verbunden. Gleichzeitig romantisch verklärt wird die Dornranke eines Rosenbusches in der Welt der Märchen und lythen, in der sie als unüberwindbare und nur durch Edelmut ezwingbare Mauer beschrieben wird oder als Zeichen für ugend und das ewige Leben. Und obwohl die Rose sinnbildlich ir Schönheit und Liebe steht und sie gesellschaftlich generell den uf der Romantikerin unter den Blumen genießt (und sich demch auch kapitalistisch verwerten lässt), sind diese positiven onnotationen der Blüte und nicht der Ranke des Rosenbusches orbehalten. Deckungsgleich verhält es sich in der griechischen ythologie, in der die rote Rose Aphrodite, der Göttin der Schönit und der Liebe, zugeschrieben ist, während die Dornen für ren inneren Schmerz stehen. Möglicherweise stehen sich Liebe und Leid aber auch unmittelbar gegenüber?

essen Trauer wird hier beschrieben? In der Alltäglichkeit des ckers findet sich eine beruhigende Normalität wieder, eine chvollziehbarkeit, die einen Bezug zur (eigenen) Gefühlswelt lässt. Und die entgegen der dornigen Wehrhaftigkeit, die von ßen gefährlich und undurchdringbar, wenn nicht sogar isorend erscheint, dennoch zeigt, dass seichter Schmerz und fte Trauer ebenso besonders wie nachvollziehbar und in gleiem Maße Normalität wie Ausnahmezustand sind. Und neben alledem auch schützenswert?

(nervous dust)

greifbar und glatt, fast erotisch scheint es, als würde alles strahlenden Rot der Dornenranke abperlen. Die Farbe, die ke und Macht symbolisiert, umgibt die Dornenranke mit r unerreichbaren Aura. Die kräftige und industrielle Farbig irritiert im Zusammenspiel mit der natürlichen Form und lässt diese dennoch vollständig wirken.

Der Abguss unter der leuchtend roten Farbe entsteht in einem aufwendigen Prozess, dessen Ergebnis bis zuletzt ungewiss ist. Während der Direktausschmelzung zerfällt die Dornenranke unter der Einwirkung extremer Hitze und über Stunden (für das Verschwinden und Auflösen ins Nichts letztlich ein relativ kurzer Zeitraum), zurück bleibt die reine Negativform in einer Hülle. Das Formgebende geht verloren, es entsteht ein Hohlkörper, der mit Bronze aufgefüllt wird. Das Verfahren kann nicht wiederholt werden, denn das (verlorene) Modell existiert nicht mehr.

Es drängt sich eine Schlussfolgerung auf: Das Verfahren ist eine Allegorie für die Vergänglichkeit des Greifbaren und Organischen sowie für das Überdauern jener unnatürlichen Form(en), die dem Modell abgenommen werden konnte(n). In diesem Sinne ist es auch ein Bild für das Verschwinden lebender Körper und dessen, was zurückbleibt, oftmals in Form von Erzählungen und Andacht. Dem Leben entnommen und eben diesem manchmal fern? Vielleicht gerade, weil hier Ephemeres genommen und für die Ewigkeit bewahrt wird. Wie entscheidet sich, welche Formen mit den daran geknüpften Geschichten in die Zukunft getragen werden? Und welche werden ausgelassen?

nervous dust [nervöser Staub] ... wie Staub, der achtlos in die Ecke gekehrt und dennoch immer wieder aufgewirbelt wird, transportieren die Sticker auf den Dornenranken Geschichten in das Hier und Jetzt. In wenigen Worten erzählen sie jene Geschichten, die in der Gegenwart passieren, nicht auf die Zukunft warten. Die kein ‚Danach' akzeptieren, die unmittelbar (und nachvollziehbar) sind und dennoch von nur wenigen erzählt werden. Geschichten, die vor Einsamkeit nicht schweigen, die über Trauer und Schmerz sprechen, die Nähe fordern und sich Zuneigung wünschen. Geschichten, deren Narrative von Verletzlichkeit handeln und von der Möglichkeit, diese zuzulassen. Es sind Geschichten, die Nachdenken ermöglichen; Geschichten über das Verschwinden, das Gehaltenwerden und das Bleiben.

(cursed)

Die chromfarbene Beschichtung umschließt die aus Bronze gegossene Dornenranke. Die Mattheit der Bronze wird aufgelöst, metallisch glänzend ist die Dornenranke über ihre Umgebung erhaben. Sie erscheint nicht nur edel, sie ist es auch. Die spiegelnde Oberfläche lässt keinen Zweifel an ihrer Wertigkeit, und die Abwehrhaltung der Dornen scheint in ihrem metallischen Glanz. Wie bereits beschrieben, bedeutet Abwehr auch Schutz, bedeuten Dornen eine unüberwindbare Hülle für einen verletzlichen Kern.

Wer mit einem Fluch belegt wird, so der Glaube in zahlreichen Überlieferungen und Geschichten, ist diesem schutzlos ausgeliefert. Denn wer verflucht ist, weiß oftmals weder von wem noch warum. Flüche sind schwer zu durchbrechen, denn sie treffen jenen Kern, den es zu schützen gilt. *cursed* [verflucht] beschreibt also einen Zustand, der unkontrolliert ist, der nur schwer beeinflusst werden kann, der sich oftmals dem eigenen Handlungsspielraum entzieht. Gleichzeitig haftet dem Fluch etwas Dunkles, Übernatürliches an, das sich nicht in weltliche Vorstellungen einordnen lässt. Wer verflucht scheint, rückt oftmals an den Rand der Gesellschaft, wirkt vereinzelt, wird isoliert. Wer sich als von der Gesellschaft abgekapselt erlebt, kann daraus Stärke ziehen, Wehrhaftigkeit entwickeln, sich neu verorten.

Vielleicht ist es die Alltäglichkeit eines Stickers, in der Trost liegen kann. Eine Alltäglichkeit, die nicht bewertet, sondern zugänglich und nachvollziehbar ist. Eine Nachvollziehbarkeit, die ebenso erhaben wie bedrohlich, natürlich wie verstörend und greifbar wie glatt sein kann. Und keinen Unterschied macht zwischen Rot. Chrom. Bronze.

Gefäße geistiger Löcher

Cathrin Mayer

„Der Tod", sagte Martin während unseres Zoom-Gesprächs, „ist der uninteressanteste Teil meiner Arbeit."

Die folgenden Kapitel, „Hermetik", „Traurige Lieder" und „Sprachlosigkeit" versuchen, über eine Art systematischen Ansatz auf das Thema der Sprache in seiner Praxis einzugehen. Anders als eine detaillierte wissenschaftliche Analyse erforscht dieser Text mithilfe der Kapitel eine Reihe von Themen, Kunstwerken und persönlichen Assoziationen.

Hermetik

Vielleicht absorbiert die Farbe Schwarz nicht nur Licht, sondern auch Sprache.

In seiner Einzelausstellung *Nervous Dust* (2022) zeigte Martin biegsame, synthetische Schläuche, die schlaff an einer Aluminiumstange hingen. *Untitled (After All 1+2)* (2019/2020) ist aus Schrumpfschlauch gefertigt, ein thermoplastisches Material, das sich unter Hitzeeinwirkung zusammenzieht und üblicherweise für Elektroisolationen und zum Schutz beschädigter Drähte und Kabel verwendet wird. Martin formt mit den Schrumpfschläuchen echte Birkenzweige ab, die in Folge wie leblose, hohle Schalen oder Häute wirken und sich auch so anfühlen. Sie wurden präzise abgelöst und beinhalten von einem lebenden Baum übriggebliebene Rindenteile.

Ich möchte anhand der Idee des Schrumpfschlauches oder eben anhand des Vorgangs, bei dem ein Objekt sehr fest eingehüllt und umschlossen wird, auf die hermetischen Aspekte von Martins künstlerischer Arbeit eingehen. Das Wort „hermetisch" bezeichnet im praktischen Sinn zum Beispiel das Isolieren eines Objektes von äußeren Einflüssen, wenn etwas also von der äußeren Umgebung abgeschottet wird. Natürlich sind die Arbeiten nicht im wörtlichen Sinn von ihrer Umgebung abgeschottet, aber sie zeichnen sich durch einen Sinn für Verinnerlichung aus. Seine architektonischen Konstruktionen arbeiten etwa mit Plastikverpackungen, mit der vorher Graberde verpackt war. Diese Konstruktionen, man könnte sie als Displays bezeichnen, bilden innerhalb der Präsentationsräume zeitliche Einheiten und ermöglichen dadurch ein intimes Wahrnehmen. Schwarze Folie erinnert an den Boden, der die Toten von den Lebenden trennt. Auch hier ruft die Farbe eine Kälte hervor, die das meiste, wenn nicht sogar das gesamte Licht schluckt. Sie verwandelt eingehende Energie in Wärme.

Sie versuchten mich zu beerdigen, aber sie wussten nicht, dass ich ein Samen bin.
Sinéad O'Connor

In Martins Oeuvre gibt es auch eine Reihe von Arbeiten, die das Licht nicht absorbieren, sondern reflektieren, und sich dabei mit einer weniger technischen Auslegung des Adjektivs „hermetisch" befassen. Sie stehen vielmehr mit der Bedeutung des Substantivs Hermetik, oder Hermetismus, in Zusammenhang.

Diese philosophische und spirituelle Tradition geht auf das Alte Ägypten zurück und wird der mythischen Figur des Hermes Trismegistus zugeschrieben. Der Kerngedanke der Hermetik ist die Existenz eines versteckten, heiligen Wissens, das in der Lage ist, die Natur der Wirklichkeit sowie das Göttliche zu offenbaren. Dieses Wissen, das oft *Corpus Hermeticum* [hermetischer Körper] genannt wird, umfasst eine Reihe von Schriften und Lehren zu verschiedenen metaphysischen und mystischen Konzepten. Die Hermetik basiert auf einem Korrespondenz-Prinzip, das davon ausgeht, dass es Verbindungen und Ähnlichkeiten zwischen Mikrokosmos (Mensch) und Makrokosmos (Universum) gibt. Wie oben, so unten – die Strukturen des Himmels spiegeln sich im irdischen Leben wider. Die Alchemie ist ein integraler Bestandteil der Hermetik. Ihr Ziel ist es, unedle Metalle in Gold zu verwandeln; eine Allegorie für spirituelle Transformation und Selbstermächtigung. Zum Prozess der Alchemie gehört die Reinigung, Auflösung und Integration des Selbst. Die Hermetik hatte einen bedeutenden Einfluss auf die Entwicklung der westlichen Esoterik, des Okkultismus und einiger Aspekte des Renaissance-Denkens. Im Laufe der Geschichte fanden ihre Ideen Eingang in eine Reihe von mystischen Traditionen und Geheimbünden. Mit der Entwicklung einzelner Glaubenssysteme entstanden Codes, die sich auf etwas jenseits der physischen Welt beziehen. Diese Codes sind immer noch lebendig, weil sie trotz aller Widerstände ahistorisches Denken und eine mythische Konstruktion des Selbst infrage stellen.

Der Künster James Lee Byars etwa griff im Zuge seiner ständigen Suche nach Sinn mythologische Bezüge auf, um sie für seinen eigenen Ansatz zu adaptieren. Unter Verwendung spezieller Materialen konstruierte er kryptische Konzepte des Perfekten, um die Unlesbarkeit einer Welt zu untersuchen, deren Materialismus jegliche Erwägung des Heiligen abzulehnen scheint. Seine Arbeit *The Rose Table of Perfect* (1989), zum Beispiel, ist eine runde Skulptur mit einem Durchmesser von 100 cm, die aus 3,333 frischen roten Rosen besteht, die im Laufe der Ausstellung langsam verwelken.

Dreiundzwanzig Jahre zuvor, im Sommer 1966, besuchte der Künstler Paul Thek mit seinem Geliebten, dem Fotografen Peter Hujar die Kapuzinergruft von Palermo, wo ihn die „8000 Leichen, die wie Blumen den Raum dekorieren", tief beeindruckten. Als Reaktion auf diese Erfahrung griff er auf die katholische Tradition der Relikte zurück. *Technological Reliquaries* (1966) besteht aus Plexiglaskästen, in denen sich Wachsrepliken von Körpern befinden.

Martins Interesse an Glaubenssystemen, verschlüsselten Praktiken und rätselhaften Ritualen zeigt sich besonders deutlich in seiner Serie von transparenten Plexiglaskästen mit Siebdrucken von eher verstörenden Bildern und Thot-Tarot-Karten von Aleister Crowley. Die Arbeit stellt zeitgenössische Reliquienschreine dar und erinnert an antike Archetypen, kunstvolle Gefäße oder Schreinbauten aus kostbaren Materialien, die, ge füllt mit Artefakten, die mit Heiligen assoziiert werden, einen visuellen Zugang zu einer spirituellen Welt bieten. Die Käste scheinen aus einer düsteren Zukunft zu stammen, in de menschliches und tierisches Leben auf wenig mehr als die ver lorenen Trümmer einer zerstörerischen Vergangenheit reduzier wurde.

Das Werk *Untitled (The Moon)* [ohne Titel (Der Mond)] (2022 zeigt das Maul eines Hundes mit einem Atemschlauch zwische den Zähnen – eine brutale Anspielung auf die Vorstellung, je manden zu verlieren, den man liebt – sowie die Tarotkarte De Mond. Die Karte zeigt Anubis, den schakalköpfigen ägypt schen Gott der Unterwelt, der die Toten durch das Jensei führt. Die Box enthält auch ein Stück Papier, auf dem ei glückskeksähnliche Botschaft zu lesen ist: „In my dreams yo don't want the best for me." [In meinen Träumen willst du nic das Beste für mich.]

Die Arbeit *Untitled (The Tower)* [ohne Titel (Der Turm)] (202 umfasst Drucke, die das Maul einer Lederschildkröte und d Tarotkarte Der Turm darstellen. Die Karte zeigt einen einsti zenden Turm und menschliche Figuren, die in den Abgru stürzen. In der rechten Ecke der Karte ist am Fuß des Bauwer ein gigantisches Paar feuerspeiender Mäuler zu sehen. Auf nem kleinen Stück Papier steht in *Untitled (The Tower)* geschr ben: „Flowers for the ones you've loved, flowers for the lost I seen." [Blumen für die, die du geliebt hast, Blumen für die V lorenen, die ich gesehen habe.] Das Maul einer Schildkr scheint auf den ersten Blick nichts Bedrohliches an sich zu ben, aber das Maul dieser besonderen Art ist völlig zahnlos u hat stattdessen so genannte „Papillen" oder „Stacheln". Papil sind scharfe, nach hinten gerichtete Stacheln, die Rachen Speiseröhre der Lederschildkröte vollständig bedecken.

Martins Plexiglaskästen stellen ein semiotisches System non baler und visueller Botschaften dar, die durch eine komm kative Verbindung mit dem Verlorenen und dem Verborge in das Aktivieren von Erinnerungen verwickelt sind. In i vermeintlichen Aufladung mit Bezügen führen sie gleichz auch in die Irre, weil sie in der Lage sind, ihre Bedeutung namisch, je nach Kontext, zu ändern. Man kann sie als psy logische Indikatoren lesen, die aus ihrem ursprünglichen Kontext gelöst wurden. Die Wörter befinden sich direkt auf den Objekten, die, weil sie sich aus einem tiefen Interesse an Symboliken und Metaphern generieren, selbst auch als eine Art Wörter in einem Gedicht fungieren, als Gefäße jenseits ihrer offensichtlichen Bedeutung. Als ästhetische und rhythmische Kompositionen verweisen sie auf eine zweite, dritte und vierte Bedeutungsebene.

Traurige Lieder

Als ich mich mit Martin über die kleinen Papierzettelchen in den Kästen unterhielt, erwähnte er *Sad Songs* [Traurige Lieder], Musikstücke, die er als Teenager oder Erwachsener hörte. Ihn faszinierte die Musik von CocoRosie und ANOHNI, und obwohl er den Liedtexten genau zuhörte, verstand er sie gelegentlich falsch.

Diese unbeabsichtigte Interpretationsform von Text offenbart jenes große Potential der Sprache, das sich nur verbal kommunizieren lässt. In *Oralität und Literalität: Die Technologisierung des Wortes* (1987; orig. 1982) untersucht der Medientheoretiker Walter J. Ong die tiefgreifenden Auswirkungen von Kommunikationstechnologien, vor allem den Übergang von der mündlichen zur schriftlichen Sprache, auf das menschliche Denken sowie auf Kultur und Bewusstsein.

> *Gänzlich schriftkundige Personen haben große Schwierigkeiten sich vorzustellen, wie eine primär orale Kultur aussieht, also eine Kultur, die weder schriftliche Grundlagen noch die Möglichkeit der Schriftlichkeit hat. Versuchen Sie sich eine Kultur vorzustellen, in der niemand jemals etwas „nachgeschlagen" hat. In einer primär oralen Kultur ist der Ausdruck „etwas nachschlagen" eine leere Phrase, er würde keinen begreifbaren Sinn ergeben. Ohne Schrift haben Wörter als solche keine visuelle Präsenz, selbst wenn die Objekte, die sie repräsentieren, visuell sind. Sie sind Klänge. Man kann sie vielleicht „abrufen" – „in Erinnerung rufen". Aber man kann sie nirgends „nachschauen". Sie haben keinen Fokus und keine Spur (eine visuelle Metapher, in der sich die Abhängigkeit von der Schrift zeigt), nicht einmal eine Richtung. Sie sind Ereignisse.*[1]

enken wir also an die oben genannten Lieder und betrachten sie als Ereignisse.

h entdeckte CocoRosie und ANOHNI in meinen frühen wanzigern. Wenn ich an diese Zeit meines Lebens zurückden- , wird mir bewusst, wie wichtig Musik damals war. Sie war ne Möglichkeit, den eigenen Geschmack auszudrücken und ente neben anderen Möglichkeiten, sich von anderen abzu- enzen, auch dazu, eine gewisse Expertise und Ahnung in Sa- en Underground-Musik zu demonstrieren. In den Laden zu hen und CDs zu kaufen war, wie auf einen Flohmarkt zu ge- n und einzigartige Schätze zu finden, die niemand außer ei- m selbst oder höchstens ein kleiner Kreis von Freund*innen nnte. Schon damals war ich fasziniert von der Rolle, die nst in CocoRosies Werk spielte. Sierra und Bianca Cassady uchten den Erzählungen ihrer naiven Lieder Leben ein, in- n sie sich als Märchengestalten verkleideten und mit Colla- Collagen arbeiteten, die sie an die Rückwand ihrer Konzert- hnen projizierten. Obwohl ihre Sprache und die Bühnen- ren naiv wirkten, waren ihre Performances voll von eroti- en Fantasien und feministischen Ideen. Diese eskapistischen lten haben mich sehr angezogen und ich war fasziniert von Biancas weiblich-maskuliner Erscheinung.

nals konnte ich diese Faszination nicht in Worte fassen, sie g über ihre Musik und Kunst hinaus und berührte etwas in mir, von dem ich nicht wusste, dass es existiert.

Heute würde ich es als eine Art Queerness *avant la lettre* bezeichnen.

Wenn ich heute an ANOHNI denke, kommt mir das Cover des Albums *I Am a Bird Now* (2005) in den Sinn: ein Portrait von Peter Hujar von Candy Darling, Warhol-Superstar und transgender Ikone, auf ihrem Totenbett. Peter Hujar (1934–1987) war ein US-amerikanischer Fotograf, der für seine stimmungsvollen schwarz-weiß Portraits und dokumentarischen Bilder bekannt ist. Berühmt wurde er in den 1970er und 1980er Jahren, als er in New York die pulsierenden und vielfältigen LGBTQIA+ und künstlerischen Communities dieser Zeit fotografierte. Hujars Fotografien befassen sich häufig mit Themen wie Sterblichkeit, Schönheit und dem menschlichen Dasein; er war stark von der klassischen Kunst und Literatur beeinflusst. Nach wie vor wird seine Arbeit für ihre rohe emotionale Kraft, die einfühlsame Darstellung von marginalisierten Personen und die einsichtsvolle Dokumentation des städtischen Wandels gefeiert. Trotz seines frühen Todes an AIDS-bedingten Komplikationen bleiben Peter Hujars Vermächtnis und sein Einfluss als bedeutende Persönlichkeit in der Geschichte der Fotografie bestehen.

Ich selbst lernte mehr über Hujar, während ich an einer großen Ausstellung über David Wojnarowicz arbeitete, ein Künstler und Aktivist, der ebenfalls an AIDS-bedingten Komplikationen starb. Damals las ich ein Buch, das zu einem meiner Lieblingsbücher wurde, *Gentrification of the Mind* (2012) von Sarah Schulman, eine US-amerikanische Autorin und Aktivistin, die für ihre Beiträge zu queerer Literatur und ihr Eintreten für LGBTQIA+-Rechte bekannt ist.

In dem Buch untersucht sie, wie die AIDS-Epidemie, die Entwicklung der Immobilienbranche und die politischen Kräfte New York City während der 1980er und 1990er Jahre prägten und zum Verschwinden verschiedener Communities und der queeren künstlerischen Subkulturen führte. Gleichzeitig plädiert sie für den Erhalt von einzigartigen Räumen und der kollektiven Erinnerung im Kontext von urbaner Homogenisierung. Die Autorin legt ein besonderes Augenmerk auf das East Village, das in den 1970er und 1980er Jahren als lebendiges und kulturell vielfältiges Viertel für seine Bohème- und Gegenkulturszene bekannt war. Das Viertel wurde von der HIV/AIDS-Epidemie der 1980er Jahre hart getroffen und ein Zentrum der Krise, mit einer hohen Zahl an HIV/AIDS-bedingten Erkrankungen und Todesfällen. Nachdem sich der Staat weigerte, für die Kranken zu sorgen und sie aus der Gesellschaft ausschloss, mussten viele die Stadt verlassen und zu ihren Familien oder Freund*innen ziehen, um gepflegt und umsorgt zu werden und zu sterben. In der Folge veränderte sich die Demografie des East Village. Die einst erschwinglichen Mieten und die verlassenen Orte des Viertels zogen wohlhabenderes Publikum und Bauunternehmen an, die aus der zentralen Lage Kapital schlagen wollten. Der Zustrom vermogenderer Personen änderte die Bevölkerungsstruktur sowie die Kultur der Gegend und verdrängte viele der dort langjährig Ansässigen und Kunstschaffenden, die es sich nicht mehr leisten konnten, dort zu leben.

Sprachlosigkeit

> *Trauer ist eine grausame Art der Erziehung. Man lernt, wie unsanft das Trauern sein kann, wie voller Wut. Man lernt, wie oberflächlich sich Kondolenzen anfühlen können. Man lernt, wie sehr Trauer mit Sprache zu tun hat, dem Scheitern von Sprache und dem Greifen nach Sprache.*
> Chimamanda Ngozi Adichie, *Notes on Grief* (2021)

Sosehr ich auch versuche, Martins Arbeiten zu analysieren, Worte für die Art und Weise zu finden, wie sie arbeiten, ich stoße immer wieder an einen Punkt der Frustration. Ich glaube, Wörter prallen von den Arbeiten ab. In *Against Interpretation* (1964) plädiert Susan Sonntag für eine „Erotik der Kunst", bei der es in erster Linie darum geht, die sinnlichen und emotionalen Qualitäten der künstlerischen Arbeit zu erleben und wertzuschätzen. Sie spricht sich für einen direkteren und instinktiveren Zugang zur Kunst aus, der dem Publikum ein emotionales und intuitives Reagieren erlaubt.

1
Walter J. Ong, *Orality and Literacy: The Technologizing of the World* (New York, Routledge, 2002) S.31. Hier dt. von der Übersetzerin

Vielleicht liegt die Erotik von Martins Arbeit in ihrem hermetischen Charakter. Sie scheinen weniger zu mir als Betrachterin zu sprechen als zueinander, wie ein System oder eine Logik von Referenzen. Jedes Objekt befindet sich dabei in einem bestimmten Bedeutungsrahmen. Im Zentrum von Martins Arbeiten scheint die Weigerung zu liegen, eindeutig auf eine bestimmte Weise gelesen zu werden – ein Widerstand gegen die Interpretation. Dies mag mit seiner ambivalenten Kombination von Bildern, Objekten und Wörtern zusammenhängen. Der fragmentarische Zugang basiert auf dem Effekt, einen Ausschnitt oder ein Stück aus einem größeren Ganzen herauszulösen. Der Glaube an etwas darüber hinaus Begreifbares verwischt die klare Linie der eindeutigen Definitionen. Aber diese Fragmente suchen nie nach Bestätigung einer Definition, sondern sind immer mit der Gefahr ihrer möglichen Auflösung beschäftigt. Sie tauchen wie unheimliche Symptome des Fehlens oder des Ausgeschlossenseins auf. Deshalb weigern sie sich auch gegen alles Direkte.

Trotz ihrer hermetischen Erscheinung bergen sie das Weiche und Sensible und lassen an Nähe und Verletzlichkeit denken. Martins Installationen und Skulpturen entfalten seelische Räume, die von innigen Erinnerungen und vermeintlich vertrauten Berührungen durchdrungen sind. Seine Arbeiten bieten keine rationalen Lösungen an für die Themen, mit denen sie sich befassen. Im Kontext dieser spannungsreichen Gegensätze evozieren sie persönliche Mythologien. Als isolierte Gefäße ihrer eigenen Möglichkeiten erschaffen sie einen poetischen Raum, der unkenntlich nach innen wie nach außen agiert und das einzigartige Drama des Selbst durchdringt.

Vielleicht ist der Geschmack von Trauer auch sanft.

Stalactite Kiss
Alex Bennett

„Der Mond hat ein Teilgesicht, er kann uns nicht
anders als so ansehen,
und ein anderes Gesicht, das immer wegschaut.
[…]
Blick' über den See und sieh', ob du mich erkennst.
Geh' durch den Nebel, bis wir uns berühren."[1]

Etwas, das mit der gegebenen Zeit seine Abwesenheit bemerkbar macht, weil es nicht wirklich empfindet. Die muschelartigen Risse des Obsidian, die hauchdünnen Einlagerungen des Phantomquarz: du bist dir selbst eine stille, dunkle Form, in der du Formen erkennst. Pausiere, um deine Hand auf das Eis zu halten. Das Frieren verwirbelt in sich selbst, klares Eis auf klarem Eis ist ein Rausch aus Ranken und Rissen, wo die weißesten Weiße in Wahrheit kleinere Splitter sind, kristallene Zweige, die Arabesken schreiben. So wie Raureifmuster auf der Haut – Lichtenbergfiguren – durch Blitzeinschläge entstehen. „Staubfiguren", „Hautfedern" oder „Lichtblumen" werden sie genannt. Mit seinem Geflecht aus gebrochenen Brüchen entlarvt das Eis jegliche Lesbarkeit als ein bloßes Scheinrelief. Wie in Dunkelheit löst sich seine Vielfalt verloren und spröde zitternd in der Tiefe auf. Schwarze Aquarellfarbe, die einem in Wasser getauchten Pinsel ausfließt. Formen der Leere, an die man sich halten möchte; eine Kälte, die erst tödlich ist und sich mit der Berührung langsam erwärmt.

Es stimmt: „So viele Dinge geben sich erst in der Abwesenheit zu erkennen."[2] Ich spreche von der tiefen Tiefe, dem Verborgenen. Die Leerstellen sind zeitlich unauflösbare Bekenntnisse, wir sind hoffnungslos an sie gebunden, weil sie den dissonanten Gedanken vorübergehend Ruhe bieten. Die Lücke ist als Raum für provisorische Entlastung gemacht. Diese Anonymität. In ihrer Extremform bekommen die Dinge andere Texturen und somit andere Resonanzen. In der Dunkelheit zum Beispiel tauchen gerade erst durch ihre Unbestimmtheit Dinge auf. Nachtgedanken. Die Abkehr von der philosophischen Dunkelheit suggeriert, dass die Zeit stehengeblieben ist, aber hier ist sie eher elliptisch. Hinfällige Materialität, beschädigtes Leitvermögen, kastrierte Futurität. Neue Materialien gebären neue Mystizismen. Wie in Rinden geritzte Herzenglyphen sind die traurigen, fast doomsdayartigen Zeichensetzungen die zaghaften Zeugen der erhofften Permanenz: Die *sanfte Trauer* des Regenwassers. Der Regen mit seinem zittrigen Versprechen, wie er tingelt und einbricht. Tatsächlich gibt der Regen ein schwereloses Gefühl, gleichzeitig ist alles verdichtet und zersplittert und sein Gefühl von Schutz macht uns zum bloßen Effekt. Man fühlt sich variabel. Der Regen formt und verformt diese vielfältige, flüchtige Dichte in uns; und ich glaube, deshalb fühlen sich die Leute „befreit".

„Ein dunkles Kleid aus Obsidian liegt über unseren wertvollsten, geheimsten Gedanken."[3] Ja, diese Psychologie verhüllt sich in Mänteln, spirituell derart dünnlich, dass die Lethargie der Dunkelheit zu einer Frage der Klimatologie wird. In der Dunkelheit bestehen wir fort: „Dunkelheit ist der Horror einer schwebenden Oasis, die das Leben ist."[4] Dieser Geist schwelgt in eiförmigen Träumereien unter einem absterbenden Himmel, durchdringt, als Atmosphäre, die Umgebung und sieht eine Welt voller träumerischer Haltungen. Du hältst dein Ohr an die interesselose Welt im Wissen, dass ihre undurchsichtige Macht sich selbst etwas verweigert. Weniger die „geistige Ejakulation"[5] der Sonne als das Verstecken ihrer Verdunkelung, die Offenlegung ihres Aufgebens. Solche einsamen Versenkungen sind heute selten, aber für diejenigen unter uns, die ähnlich entfremdet sind, hat es sie immer gegeben. Man hegt Sympathien für eine Welt ohne uns, und für die kosmische Negativität, die uns überdauern wird.

„Überwuchert werden wie eine Ruine."[6] Diese Überreste zeugen von dem, was einmal war, von Dingen, die auf keine einfache Art verloren gehen können. Zwiespältig streifen sie die Welt der *reliquiae,* geben sich aber mit deren verkalkter Endlichkeit nicht zufrieden. Ihr anti-vanitas Vibe erfreut sich an der Feierlichkeit des Übriggebliebenen und an der Besonnenheit von Schutt. Jedes der düsteren Gefäße suggeriert eine Fiktion des Eingeschlossenseins, während sie in Wahrheit das Intrasubjektive eröffnen. Das Innere ist fast radikal hautlos geworden, geröntgt und durchsichtig. Rätselhafte Rätsel, deren gebleckte Zähne und blinde, gnadenlose Augen den Kontakt suchen. Dieser innere Geist, ohne Körper, ist potent genug um als Beschreiber dessen zu fungieren, was nicht da ist – eine unendliche Abwesenheit, in der es keine angemessene Sprache gibt und jegliches philosophische Denken zusammenbricht. Endlich: Wir sind alle offen verschlüsselt, füreinander, für uns selbst. Exquisite, entzweite Hoffnungslosigkeit. Die entblößten Umrisse des einzelnen Subjekts lösen sich im Onyxdunkel einer grellen Leere auf. Dieser offene Tiefschlafzustand der Beziehung zwischen Selbst und Welt ist eine Einladung für eine Intimität der privaten Symbolismen. Wenn es sich dabei um einen Weg handelt, die Welt auf gleiche Weise zu betrachten wie einen individuellen Körper, oder einen Gedanken, dann handelt es sich um eine pessimistische Entgrenzung von Psyche und Welt. „Ein Solipsismus, der auch eine ultimative Form von Empathie mit dem Nichtmenschlichen darstellt. Die einzige Fantasie, die sich der Pessimismus erlaubt – die Traurigkeit des Kosmos."[7]

Unverortbar; die Zeit ist hier in der Schwebe, die Formen scharen sich um ein verwaistes Gefühl von „danach", von Verlust, der genau wie bei der Melancholie nicht lokalisierbar ist. Bei Melancholie lässt sich kein Verlust festmachen; er wurde ausgeblendet und seine Wiederherstellung scheinbar ins Unendliche verschoben.

Eingerollt richtet sich der abgetrennte, melancholische Blick nach innen, weil die Silhouette, die man ausfüllen möchte, einfach unbekannt ist und ihr Verlustobjekt nur zur Hälfte am Leben. Walter Benjamin sieht in der Melancholie keinen Widerspruch zur Trauer, weniger sei sie ein pathologischer Zustand als eine aktive Haltung, die einen Verlust symbolisch nach innen kehrt und zur Ruhe bringt. In dieser Arbeit, „vom Feld des Betrauerns hin zu dem der Bedeutung", wie Ilit Ferber schreibt, drückt sich „eine Vertiefung des Verlustes aus, eine weitere Abtötung des Objekts, aus dem eine Fülle entsteht."[8] Der Verlust wird erhalten und intensiviert, anstatt entfernt und überwunden. In Hinblick auf ihre Möglichkeiten und in Anlehnung an Ferbers Analyse von Benjamins melancholischem Engagement, könnte man diese Arbeiten als Ansammlungen von Ablösungen verstehen, die mittels *Expression* das Verlustobjekt *präsent* machen wollen. „Folglich", schreibt Ferber, „bedeutet die Ablösung hier ein Zeigen, und nicht ein Verheimlichen oder Unterdrücken."[9] In diesem Zustand des vollen Ausdrucks wird das Objekt dem Leben entzogen … stillgelegt, abgetötet, begraben, eingefroren. Es sind diese kleinen, in den Zustand des völligen Stillstandes gebrachten Tode, die wir sammeln.

1
T Fleischmann, *Time Is the Thing a Body Moves Through* (Minneapolis: Coffee House Press, 2019), S. 97. Hier dt. von der Übersetzerin.
2
Ibid., 37.
3
Eugene Thacker, *Infinite Resignation* (London: Repeater Books, 2018), S. 59. Hier dt. von der Übersetzerin.
4
Eugene Thacker, *Cosmic Pessimism* (Minneapolis: Univocal Publishing, 2015), S. 21. Hier dt. von der Übersetzerin.
5
Georges Bataille, *Visions of Excess* (Minneapolis: University of Minnesota Press, 1970; 1985), S. 57. Hier dt. von der Übersetzerin.
6
Thacker, *Cosmic Pessimism*, S. 54. Hier dt. von der Übersetzerin.
7
Thacker, *Infinite Resignation*, S. 66. Hier dt. von der Übersetzerin.
8
Ilit Ferber, „Melancholy Philosophy: Freud and Benjamin", *EREA* 4.1 (Spring 2006), S. 66–74. Hier dt. von der Übersetzerin.
9
Ibid.

In den Nachwehen dieser erstarrten, versuchsweise auf Distanz gehaltenen Formen liegt die prozessuale Melancholie mit ihrer abgelegten Zerrissenheit, was sich ebenfalls Ferbers „vertieftem Tod" zuschreiben ließe. Entfremdung und Disharmonie bleiben ungelöst und werden in der Erinnerung ausgelegt wie vorgebildete Wunden. Die Arbeit besteht in dieser Selbst-Welt im Beobachten der Möglichkeiten am Punkt ihrer Sinnentleerung. Am zwecklosen Punkt der Frage: *Was bleibt?* In den leeren Dimensionen spalten sich tiefe Eindrücke auf.

Diese Überlegungen sind sicher eine Bemühung um Nähe, um in den eigenen Mängeln verlorene Dinge aufzuspüren und durch das Schreiben die vielen brachliegenden und nachklingenden Gedanken, Bilder und Intimitäten einzuhegen. Die Suche nach dem Nachklang des Eigenen im Anderen ist ein beidseitig irreponibles Unterfangen – ich nehme die Gedanken von Moyra Davey: „Ich bin auf die Gedanken von anderen angewiesen und ich klammere mich an die Toten."[10] Stalagmitartige Anhänge in einem System von Echos, die „so vielen Dinge" des Fehlens. In solchen Momenten ergründen wir uns selbst genauso wie jemanden anderen. Das wiederholte Scheitern, jemanden anderen zu verinnerlichen, richtet immer wieder die „Wünsche" und das „Begehren" aus, und selbst auf die Gefahr hin, erneute Verluste zu erleiden, wendet man sich ihnen immer wieder zu – ein Prozess, der paradoxerweise das Gefühl des Am-Leben-Seins verstärkt. Das sind die merkwürdigen Forderungen intimer Distanzen – die womöglich immer wieder neue Aufnahmen und Annahmen benötigen. Die Sehnsucht nach dem unmöglichen „ohne", nach nichtmenschlichen Gedanken und nach einer abgelegenen Kontinuität, dort, wo der Mond wegsieht – erst dort in der atmosphärischen Landschaft der Innerlichkeit werde ich gesehen, und trete durch den Nebel hindurch in Beziehung.

10
Moyra Davey, *Index Cards* (London: Fitzcarraldo Editions, 2020), S. 188. Hier dt. von der Übersetzerin.

Nervous Dust
Vincent Schier

Ausgangspunkt für die Publikation *Nervous Dust* ist die gleichnamige Einzelausstellung von Martin Maeller im Kunstverein Göttingen im Jahr 2022. Die Publikation bietet den ersten, umfangreichen Überblick über sein künstlerisches Schaffen und seine intensive und beharrliche Auseinandersetzung mit Erfahrungen von Verlust, Entfremdungsprozessen und der Suche nach Zugehörigkeit. Durch die Beiträge von Autor*innen und Künstler*innen werden tiefergehende Einblicke in Themenfelder gegeben, die in Martins künstlerischer Arbeit erkennbar sind. Es werden Perspektiven in Martins Arbeit aufgezeigt, die Kontexte und Gedanken auf facettenreiche Art bündeln und sich auf kritische Weise entfalten.

Martins Arbeit kombiniert persönliche Erfahrungen, Text und Elemente der Pop- und Subkultur, um subjektive und kollektive Zustände psychischer und physischer Grenzerfahrungen zu beobachten. Seine Arbeit erstreckt sich über verschiedene Medien wie Druckgrafik, Skulpturen und Installationen und erschafft innere Welten zwischen Melancholie und Verlust, Zuneigung und Fürsorge. Seine visuelle und konzeptionelle Sprache präsentiert flüchtige Momente, die Räume der Resonanz für individuelles Bewusstsein bilden.

Er entfremdet und fragmentiert übersehene und unkonventionelle Objekte, verwandelt sie und verleiht ihnen eine neue Bedeutung. Seine Werke sind häufig mit kunst- und kulturhistorischen Verweisen aufgeladen und wirken glatt und reduziert, aber auch intim und intuitiv. Durch die Verwendung von industriellen und organischen Materialien sowie persönlichen und anonymen Objekten schaffen Martins Werke scheinbar unheimliche Atmosphären, in denen ein Gefühl der Vertrautheit selten zu finden ist.

Auf poetische Art und Weise hinterfragt Martin, wie Identität konstruiert wird und betont dabei die ihr innewohnende Sensibilität und Verletzlichkeit. Er verwischt die Vorstellungen von gesellschaftlichen Konventionen und verweist mitunter auf diejenigen, die sich aufgrund ihrer eigenen Identität von der Welt abgekapselt fühlen. Seine Arbeit berührt queere Kultur, Machtstrukturen und die Beziehung zwischen Mensch und Natur. Sie eröffnen einen spirituellen Bereich, der kaum greifbar im Unheimlichen verbleibt. Sie bringen unangepasste Formen des Erinnerns und Gedenkens hervor, die im Kontrast zur physischen Welt stehen. Die künstlerische Arbeit hinterfragt und reflektiert, was einen persönlichen Wert hat und was im kollektiven Gedächtnis gespeichert wird.

Martin formuliert immer wieder Narrationen, die bewusst Widersprüche erzeugen. Durch die Integration individueller Codes und loser Definitionen lenkt er die Aufmerksamkeit auf ambivalente Momente und schafft so Orte der Kraft. Seine Skulpturen und Installationen konzentrieren sich auf innere, unentdeckte Welten, die aufgrund von Ablehnung oder Verdrängung außerhalb gängiger Betrachtungsweisen liegen. Mit seiner künstlerischen Arbeit dechiffriert und kartografiert er so das dunkle Terrain des Unbewussten und fokussiert sich auf die Rückgewinnung der persönlichen Handlungsmacht.

Diese Publikation ist das Ergebnis einer intensiven, aber vor allem engagierten und engen Zusammenarbeit. Martin und ich danken allen Beteiligten, insbesondere Samuel Bänziger, der die richtige Form für diese Publikation gefunden hat. Dank an Danny Rogers für die Erstveröffentlichung ihres Gedichts Seafoam aus dem Jahr 2022 und an P. Staff für den poetischen Beitrag, der speziell für diese Publikation fertiggestellt wurde. Dank auch an Alex Bennett für den Beitrag, der die emotionale Dunkelheit erhellt und dazu ermutigt, Licht auf ihre verschleierte Schönheit zu werfen. Vielen Dank an Philipp Hindahl für die sorgfältig gewählten Worte, die den Melancholiker nicht enttäuschen und Cathrin Mayer für die präzisen Formulierungen und Gedanken zu Martins Werk. Wir bedanken uns bei allen für das Vertrauen in dieses Projekt.

List of Works

3 untitled (darkness say my name), detail
4 untiteld (darkenss say my name)
silkscreen on pmma, paper
27 × 27 × 27 cm
2023
9 untitled (love note 1–4)
aluminium
approx. 54 × 25,5 × 6 cm
2023
10 untitled (love note 2)
aluminium
approx. 54 × 25,5 × 6 cm
2023
13 untitled (roses scan 9)
silkscreen on abrasive paper
92 × 119 cm
2023
14, 15 untitled (roses scan 9), detail
16–19 Installation Views
"floor is lava"
Kunsthalle Bratislava
2023
21 untitled (cursed)
chrome plated bronze, PVC
242 × 3,5 × 3,5 cm
2022
22 untitled (cursed), detail
30, 31 Installation View
"Nervous Dust"
Kunstverein Göttingen
2022
33 Installation View
"Nervous Dust"
Kunstverein Göttingen
2022
34, 35 Installation View
"Nervous Dust"
Kunstverein Göttingen
2022
36, 37 untitled (lonely nights)
silkscreen on PMMA, PVC
27 × 27 × 27 cm
2022
39 untitled (lonely nights), detail
40 untitled (roses scan 1)
silkscreen on abrasive paper
94 × 132 cm
2022
42, 43 untitled (roses scan 1), detail
45 untitled (in my dreams)
silkscreen on PMMA, paper
27 × 27 × 27 cm
2021
46, 47 untitled (in my dreams), detail
49 untitled (in my dreams), detail
50 untitled (in my dreams), detail
54, 55 Installation View
"lethargic rays"
Loggia/U26
2023
57 untitled (roses scan 61)
silkscreen on abrasive paper
135 × 98 cm
2023/2022
58, 59 untitled (roses scan 61), detail
61 untitled (roses scan 52)
silkscreen on abrasive paper
137 × 98 cm
2023/2022
62, 63 untitled (roses scan 52), detail
65 Installation View
"lethargic rays"
Loggia/U26
2023
66, 67 Installation View
"lethargic rays"
Loggia/U26
2023
68 untitled (nervous dust), detail
powder-coated bronze, PVC
240 × 3 × 3 cm
2022
73 untitled (nervous dust),
powder-coated bronze, PVC
240 × 3 × 3 cm
2022
75 untitled (the tower), detail
76, 77 untitled (the tower), detail
78 untitled (the tower)
silkscreen on PMMA, paper
27 × 27 × 27 cm
2022
81 untitled (the tower), detail
84, 85 Installation View
"Nervous Dust"
Kunstverein Göttingen
2022
86, 87 untitled (after all 1–3)
polyolefin
dimensions variable
2023-2019
89 untitled (after all 1–3), detail
90 untitled (after all 1–3), detail
97 untitled (soft sorrow), detail
98 untitled (soft sorrow)
bronze, PVC
232 × 2,5 × 2,5 cm
2022
100, 101 untitled (snake)
silkscreen on PMMA, paper
27 × 27 × 27 cm
2022/2021
103 untitled (snake), detail
104, 105 untitled (bite 3), detail
107 untitled (bite 3)
glass
22 × 7 × 19 cm
2021/2020
108 untitled (roses scan 14)
silkscreen on abrasive paper
91 × 132 cm
2023/2022
112, 113 untitled (roses scan 14), detail
114, 115 untitled (roses scan 14), detail
116 untitled (haunted house)
silkscreen on abrasive paper
27 × 27 × 27 cm
2023
119 untitled (haunted house), detail
126, 127 untitled (roses scan 14 red), detail
128, 129 untitled (roses scan 14 red), detail
131 untitled (roses scan 14 red)
silkscreen on abrasive paper
94 × 132 cm
2023
132 untitled (bite 4)
glass
21 × 22 × 7 cm
2021/2020
135 untitled (bite 4), detail
136, 137 Installation View
"lethargic rays"
Loggia/U26
2023
139 untitled (cold world), detail
140, 141 untitled (cold world)
silkscreen on PMMA, paper
27 × 27 × 27 cm
2023/2022
142 untitled (cold world), detail

Colophon / Impressum

Editor / Herausgeber
Vincent Schier / Kunstverein Göttingen

Art Direction / Gestaltung
Samuel Bänziger, Bänziger Hug

Editorial Team / Redaktion
Martin Maeller, Vincent Schier

With contributions by / Mit Beiträgen von
Alex Bennett, Philipp Hindahl, Martin Maeller, Cathrin Mayer, Bunny Rogers, Vincent Schier, P. Staff

Translation / Übersetzung
Julianne Cordray
(German – English / Deutsch – Englisch)
Lina Morawetz
(English – German / Englisch – Deutsch)

Copy Editing / Lektorat
Johanna Schindler (German / Deutsch)
Madeleine LaRue (English / Englisch)

Image Editing / Lithografie
Druckerei Kettler, Bönen/Westfalen

Photo Credits / Bildnachweise
Marlene Burz, Jan Kolský

This publication is published following the exhibition *Nervous Dust* (15 July – 28 August 2022) at Kunstverein Göttingen.
The project was supported by

Diese Publikation erscheint anschließend an die Ausstellung *Nervous Dust* im Kunstverein Göttingen (15. Juli – 28. August 2022).
Das Projekt wurde gefördert von

Niedersächsisches Ministerium für Wissenschaft und Kultur

AKB STIFTUNG

GÖTTINGEN STADT, DIE WISSEN SCHAFFT

Sparkasse Göttingen SEIT 1801

LANDSCHAFTS VERBAND SÜDNIEDERSACHSEN

Mit Unterstützung der Senatsverwaltung für Kultur und Gesellschaftlicher Zusammenhalt

kunstverein göttingen

Kunstverein Göttingen e.V.
Gotmarstraße 1
37073 Göttingen
www.kunstvereingoettingen.de

Published and distributed by
Mousse Publishing
Contrappunto s.r.l.
Via Pier Candido Decembrio 28,
20137, Milan, Italy

Available through:

Mousse Publishing, Milan
moussemagazine.it

DAP | Distributed Art Publishers, New York
artbook.com

Les presses du réel, Dijon
lespressesdureel.com

Antenne Books, London
antennebooks.com

Idea books, Amsterdam
ideabooks.nl

LibroCo, Firenze
libroco.it

First edition: 2024
Printed in Germany by Druckerei Kettler, Bönen / Westfalen
ISBN 978-88-6749-622-8
€ 25 / $ 30